Brain Friendly ReVision

Published by Network Educational Press Ltd.
PO Box 635
Stafford
ST16 1BF

First published 2002
© UFA 2002

ISBN 185539 127 9

Every effort has been make to contact copyright holders of material reproduced in this book. The publishers apologise for any omissions and will be pleased to rectify them at the earliest opportunity. Please see p.243 for a comprehensive list of acknowledgements.

Brain Friendly is the registered Trade Mark of Mark Fletcher and Richard Munns of Brain-Friendly Publications. Brain-Friendly Publications publish books and run seminars for teachers, particularly in the subject area of Modern Foreign Languages. Contact: 25 Julian Road, Folkestone, CT19 5HW. Tel: 01303 242892

Contributors: UFA National Team (Sarah Burgess, Maggie Farrar, Manjit Shellis, Lyn Reynolds)
Edited by: Carol Thompson & Peter Wrapson
Design by: Neil Hawkins
Illustrations by: Michelle Hutchings of Mary Jones Design

Printed in Great Britain by MPG Books Ltd., Bodmin, Cornwall.

Contents

You can't be that

I told them:
When I grow up
I'm not going to be a scientist
Or someone who reads the news on TV.
No, a million birds will fly through me.
I'M GOING TO BE A TREE!

They said,
You can't be that. No, you can't be that.

I told them:
When I grow up
I'm not going to be an airline pilot,
A dancer, a lawyer or an MC.
No, huge whales will swim in me.
I'M GOING TO BE AN OCEAN!

They said,
You can't be that. No, you can't be that.

I told them:
I'm not going to be a DJ,
A computer programmer, a musician or a beautician.
No, streams will flow through me, I'll be the home of eagles;
I'll be full of nooks and crannies, valleys and fountains.
I'M GOING TO BE A RANGE OF MOUNTAINS!

They said,
You can't be that. No, you can't be that.

I asked them:
Just what do you think I am?
Just a child, they said,
And children always become one of the things
We want them to be.

They do not understand me.
I'll be a stable if I want, smelling of fresh hay,
I'll be a lost glade in which unicorns still play.
They do not realise I can fulfil any ambition.
They do not realise that among them
Walks a magician.

Brian Patten

Foreword

There comes a time when all the energy that teachers have put into their teaching, the relationships they have built, the activities they have developed, the passion they have brought to their subject and the delight in learning they have tried to awaken is tested.

There comes a time for young people when the many days and hours in the classroom, the heavy bag full of books, the journey from unknowing to knowing and the many hours of questioning, discussing, reading, writing and performing are put to the test.

Of course we know that the real test of learning is how confident young people feel as they make their way in the world – how they deal with change, relationships, setbacks, success and failure and how they contribute meaningfully to their world. But there are also exams and tests along the way and great store is placed upon the results – by students, parents, teachers and schools. Part of the work of the school is to prepare young people for those tests and exams in the best possible way and, in so doing, give them habits of learning and attitudes to learning that will endure beyond school.

This book gives teachers the tools they will need to help young people to revise in a way which works with their brain and supports their own individual approach to learning. This book is designed to give young people the confidence to first of all explore how their brains work and then use that knowledge as they revise. It looks at what some of the barriers to revision might be for young people and how they might overcome them and gives them the tools they need to manage their time both prior to and during exams.

Teachers who have worked with us on these workshops have realised that there is no mystique to 'accelerated learning'. Teachers who come to training sessions on brain friendly revision and accelerated learning sometimes expect something new and strange – and instead find a philosophy and pedagogy that fits entirely with their own personal philosophy of learning. They find that the learning in these workshops is personal, individual and meaningful, just as learning should be.

We are fortunate that in the University of the First Age we have the opportunity to work with countless young people, their schools and their teachers. Whether we are working in schools in Durham, Cornwall, Norfolk, Birmingham, Leeds or London the challenge is the same. Young people want to enjoy learning and want to feel that they are successful at it. Teachers and schools are in the business of opening minds and want to do it to the very best of their ability. All have taken part in the workshops in this book and have fed back their experiences to us – the workshops we present here are shaped by their input.

Many teachers are drawn to experiment with brain based approaches to revision in a desperate attempt to 'ratchet up' their test scores in order to crawl higher up the league tables – and we know of many remarkable achievements when schools have adopted the techniques outlined in this book. These schools and young people are to be applauded, as they bear testimony to the power of accelerated brain friendly approaches. But that should never be the prime reason for opening this book and sharing it with your students. These workshops can be used at any time and in any place with young people and their teachers to help maximise the learning that goes on day in, day out in all our schools. Brain friendly revision techniques, if adopted as an integral part of learning throughout the year, can help young people to face exams and tests with more resilience, more resources and more confidence in themselves as learners.

We hope you enjoy exploring these workshops with your colleagues and students. I would like to thank the UFA national team and all the UFA National partners who have contributed to these workshops over the years.

Maggie Farrar
Director – National UFA

For more information see 'A quick guide to the UFA' pp.237–8.

Designing and leading your revision programme

The content of your revision programme depends on the length of time available and the needs of the students.

A useful starting point would be to consider the following questions:

- What are the specific needs of the students?
- What are the aims of our revision programme?
- How will I know if the programme has been a success?
- How much time do we have to deliver the programme?

Some possible models:

■ A one-week, intensive programme where the first two days are taught using the workshops from this booklet and the remaining three days comprise supported study where the students bring their personal revision and are supported by other students and tutors. This will allow them to explore the techniques taught earlier in the week and to seek help when they need it.

■ A series of workshops after school using the first three 'core' workshops followed by some of the extension workshops and/or supported study. The number of workshops will depend on how many of the techniques you want to explore, and in what depth.

■ 'Super Learning Days' for revision.
UFA 'Super Learning Days' are all about learning to learn. Staff undergo training prior to the day and students take part in workshops focusing on the process of learning run by the school staff. The aim of a Super Learning Day is to begin to open up students' minds to different ways of learning and ensure that the ways explored are practical, effective and fun. Many schools find it valuable to do a whole day with students on revision techniques – this introduces all the students and a range of staff to the techniques of brain friendly revision, which can then be followed up in class. The aims of your Super Learning Days need to be very clear. Once these have been determined, a programme can then be devised from the workshops outlined here. The Super Learning Day could also be used as a taster day followed by more in-depth workshops after school or specific techniques such as mind mapping could be followed up and reinforced in class.
In KS3 the content could reflect English, Maths and Science curricula in preparation for SATs, with revision techniques being the main focus of the day.
In KS4 exam preparation may be a more significant part of the day.

■ A revision programme might be delivered through the PHSME/tutorial structure within the school timetable. Again, the number of sessions would depend on the length of lessons and the number of techniques you want to cover and the needs of the students. You may want to supplement the programme with after-school workshops.

Leading workshops

The workshops have been planned to model accelerated learning principles and have all been written by practising teachers who have been part of the UFA Fellowship Training Programme. All of the activities in this book have been tried and tested in schools and out of hours learning centres across the UK with a wide range of students in KS3 and KS4. The core workshops provide a foundation upon which the skills and techniques in the extension workshops can be developed. All the activities in the workshops are timed to fit into the time you have available.

Each workshop comprises:

- an introductory session with background information for the tutor
- an 'at a glance' workshop plan to give the big picture of the activities in the workshop, their aims and how long each activity takes
- detailed notes for the delivery of the activities
- photocopiable resources to support activities (at the end of each workshop).
- posters (left hand pages), which can be photocopied and used as peripherals for your classroom or given to students to enrich their own revision environment

To date, these workshops have been delivered by UFA Fellows* and other teachers in their schools, who have all had UFA training to support their delivery. The guidelines on the following pages, '10 ways to make your revision sessions more brain friendly', will take tutors through suggestions for ensuring that the workshops 'walk the talk' of accelerated learning.

Notes about resources

- To make your materials more colourful we suggest that resource sheets be photocopied onto coloured paper. Use colour wherever possible – it aids memory!
- Paper and pens/pencils are not usually listed in the resources; it is assumed that these will be available.

---

* Tutors working with the UFA at an LEA and school level. See pp.237–8 for more about the UFA.

---

10 ways to make your revision sessions more brain friendly

It is important that your sessions not only teach useful techniques but also model accelerated learning. If they do, students will not only learn the techniques but also understand the importance of the processes they are undertaking, which will be a useful model for their own individual revision at home. Encourage students to adopt good revision habits!

Alistair Smith's Accelerated Learning Cycle (*Accelerated Learning in the Classroom*) is an excellent tool for planning and delivering sessions and has informed the writing of the workshops in this manual. The suggestions below are also rooted in this cycle.

1. Create a supportive, welcoming learning environment.

Young people will respond best in an environment that is challenging but safe. Make the environment as welcoming as possible both in physical and personal ways. Think about the layout of chairs and tables (if you need them). Aim to ensure that the relationships within the group are positive; if appropriate, you could perhaps make a group contract. Aim to make the learning fun! If you can, invite older students to work with you as peer tutors as this will help to make the environment more 'young person' oriented and less intimidating. Consider providing refreshments – dehydration may impair brain function, so think about providing water.

2. Make full use of the peripheral environment. Display positive statements, subject – specific vocabulary/prompts and important exam information.

Our brains take in an enormous amount of information subconsciously from the peripheral environment – so use it. Encourage students to use the peripheral environment at home too to display reminders, important quotations, mind maps etc. Draw attention to the environment whenever you can and encourage students to use it in their revision and to imagine themselves back in their revision space when they are sitting the exam so they can 'read the walls'.

3. Make sure you address the question 'what's in it for me?' for the learners at the start of every session.

We know that intrinsic motivation is very important for learning. Our minds will focus more readily on something that we see as valuable and that fits in with our own personal, long term goals. Students may be motivated if they think a session is going to be useful for their revision and ultimately for success in exams, but they may also be motivated to get involved if they think the session is going to be fun or novel. The best ambassadors for the session are those students who are benefiting from it – encourage them to share their experience with other students.

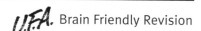 Brain Friendly Revision

4. Be clear about your aims for the session and help students to target-set.

Our brains process parts and wholes simultaneously. Whilst one brain area processes details, another processes the 'big picture'. Ensure students know what they are going to be doing during the session and outline the goals you hope to achieve in it. Encourage students to target-set for themselves too (both within your sessions and at home), as they will all have slightly different needs and therefore slightly different aims.

5. Try to meet the needs of visual, auditory and kinaesthetic learners.

Research in the field of Neuro-Linguistic Programming clearly shows that different people perceive things in different ways. If students have a range of learning styles we need to try to ensure that the activities we plan are accessible to everyone. Perhaps your own preference has an impact on how you teach? Aim to present things in visual, auditory and kinaesthetic (physical) ways.

6. Try to encourage students to use colour and images as much as possible. Try using music to aid concentration or create a particular atmosphere, or try linking it to specific content to aid recall.

One of the most effective ways of stimulating the brain is the use of colour and images. Colourful rooms invite interest and curiosity and appeal to the emotions. Try to make sure students have the resources they need to make their learning colourful and encourage them to make their own revision colourful. Music can also aid revision. It can help reduce stress and anxiety and it adds another sensory dimension to the room. It can make periods of quiet reflection more acceptable and thinking more creative. It can counteract the effects of a cold and empty environment. It can also raise energy and help to produce a state of relaxed alertness which is ideal for receptive learning. However, don't use music all the time, and be aware that some people may find it distracting. (See p.242 for suggestions of music that aids learning.)

7. Plan activities using the theory of Multiple Intelligences.

Howard Gardner's theory of Multiple Intelligences (see p.49) suggests that what's important is not how intelligent you are, but how you are intelligent. Different people learn differently. Our brains are as individual as our fingerprints and so we are likely to have different intelligence profiles, and at any time may exhibit different skills and abilities. Plan sessions to cater for different people's different intelligence strengths, but encourage students to try things out in different ways rather than always opting for what comes easily. If students approach a subject in a number of different ways, their understanding of it is more likely to be deep rather than superficial and they will have more 'memory hooks' to use to remember information.

8. Make it active.

We know that many people have a kinaesthetic preference, but movement is good for all of us. The brain is the greediest organ in the body for oxygen. It uses approximately 20 percent of the oxygen in our blood. Activity helps us to stay alert and focused. Build movement into activity as much as you can and encourage students to move around when they are revising. Use Brain Gym® and stretch breaks regularly. When students are sitting encourage them to sit up straight and breathe deeply – hunched shoulders and shallow breathing will not help them to be mentally alert when revising or studying.

9. **Build in opportunities for students to demonstrate their learning and 'show what they know'.**

Students teaching other students is a great way to do this and consolidates the learning for the one doing the teaching. Encourage students to talk out their learning to a friend or incorporate individual or group presentation as part of the session. This consolidates the learning, as the learner has to articulate their understanding to someone else. This then becomes the first opportunity to review what has been learnt.

10. **Build in regular review.**

Revision is a much less arduous task if reviewing takes place regularly. Students will find it easier to review regularly for short periods of time rather than having to cover everything just before the exams. We will remember less as time goes on. If we review regularly we halt this natural decline in our ability to remember. Encourage students to review what they have been revising; at the end of your session, at the end of the day, and again at the end of the week, and so on. Recall will happen easier and faster if this approach is adopted.

MY AMAZING BRAIN!

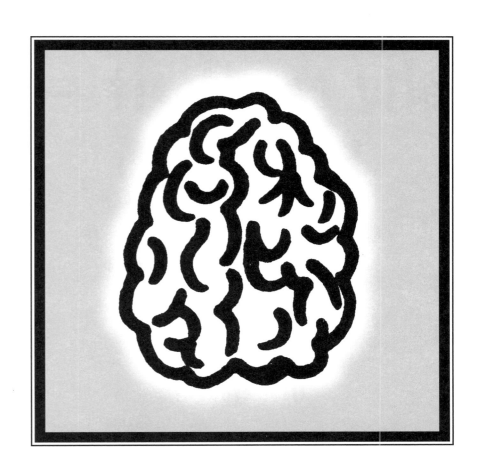

'You know, when you start to learn like this you realise that you really have got a brain and you really can do it — it helped my confidence.'

UFA student

My amazing brain!

Research into the brain is amassing at an amazing rate. New discoveries about the brain and the way that it works continue to inform our knowledge of effective learning. With a greater understanding of how we learn, how the brain responds to different stimuli, how memory works and the effects of stress on our learning, students will be better able to plan effective revision.

The activities in this workshop cover some facts about the brain and how these relate to revision.

The brain and learning

The brain has a much greater potential than is generally believed. Researchers now think that most people use no more than one percent of their brain's capacity for memory and creative thinking. Perhaps by understanding more about how our brains work, this capacity can be greatly increased. It is not that there are vast areas of our brains that we don't use, but rather that we do not make full use of its potential.

There are approximately one hundred billion neurones (100,000,000,000) in the human brain. Each one is capable of making contact with between a thousand and a hundred thousand other cells. The number of possible combinations is virtually limitless! However, we only use a tiny fraction of this potential. So, there is an enormous amount of untapped potential in each individual; everyone, no matter what their starting point, can be smarter.

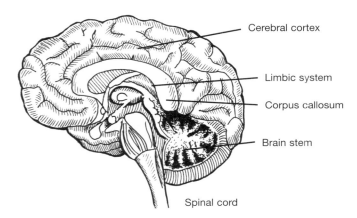

The **cerebral cortex** is split into two halves or hemispheres. Looking a bit like a walnut, this area of the brain is believed to be the most recently evolved. The level of 'folding' is thought to be associated with the level of complexity of brain function – the most complex being the human brain, which is able to function and react to a complex, ever-changing environment. Although it is overly simplistic to pinpoint where particular functions happen in particular bits of the cortex, MRI scans do show that in many people (90 percent of right handers) functions in the hemispheres are lateralised.

It is thought that the left hemisphere is primarily concerned with analytical, logical and linear thought processes, focusing on the detail of a stimulus, whilst the right hemisphere is more likely to be concerned with imagination, visual processing, creativity and music, focusing on the whole rather than the detail. We

'An idea is a new combination of old elements. There are no new elements. There are only new combinations.'

George Dryden
English poet

all have a tendency for one hemisphere to be dominant. However, the **corpus callosum**, which links the hemispheres, is thought to contain around 200 million nerve fibres, so the capacity for communication between the hemispheres is great.

All forms of learning situation need to take this into consideration; revision activities need to be created where both left and right-brain dominant participants can learn easily. It is also thought to be possible to stimulate neurones firing across the corpus callosum by doing certain exercises such as Brain Gym®.

In the mid brain there is a complex arrangement of modules known as the **limbic system**. The limbic system is thought to be important for unconscious processing but is connected to the cortex via a dense array of neurones. This part of the brain has also in the past been known as the 'mammalian' brain, because it shares many features with other mammals. It is older in evolutionary terms than the cortex. Two very important structures within the limbic system are the Hippocampus and the Amygdala. The Hippocampus seems to be essential for the laying down of memories (although how 'memory' works is still not fully understood). A recent newspaper headline: 'London cabbies have big hippocampuses' referred to research which found that taxi drivers in London had unusually large hippocampuses, thought to be linked to their amazing capacity for spatial memory. The Amygdala is also in this region and is thought to be where fear is registered. Indeed, this mid brain area is thought to be important for the processing of our emotional responses. In a learning situation much of what is taught may not be remembered unless it has some kind of emotional content. Enjoyment and feeling successful are very important elements of good revision.

The **brain stem**, located at the base of the brain, is formed from the nerves that come up via the spinal column. In evolutionary terms this is probably the most primitive part of the brain and we share some aspects of this with present day reptiles! In fact, this area used to be referred to as the 'reptilian' brain. Areas within the brain stem regulate the brain's general level of alertness and are also responsible for regulating bodily processes such as breathing, heart rate and blood pressure, things that are not under our conscious control.

When people are under stress some research suggests that this state may cause a kind of shut down effect as blood rushes to the parts of the brain that are needed for survival. This may in severe cases result in 'fight or flight' type behaviour, which is not under conscious control. When in this state, problem solving and creative thinking is difficult.

It is now widely accepted that stress inhibits learning. People learn best when they are in a state of relaxed alertness and do not feel threatened or anxious. The revision environment needs to be as stress-free for the learner as possible, whilst still providing challenge. We also need to encourage students to recognise the effects of stress on their learning and provide strategies for reducing it. Encouraging the use of Brain Gym® and other physical exercises that students can use when studying on their own will considerably enhance their general well-being as well as their ability to use their brains effectively.

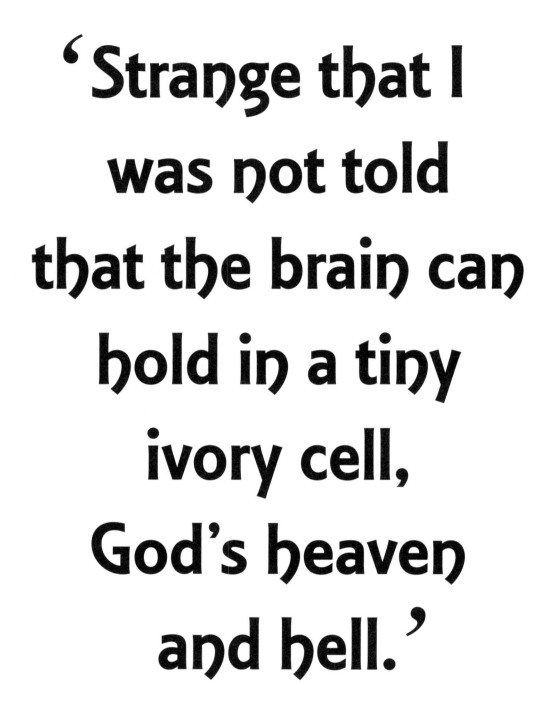

'Strange that I was not told that the brain can hold in a tiny ivory cell, God's heaven and hell.'

Oscar Wilde
Irish dramatist

Brain Gym®

Brain Gym® is a quick and effective way of changing or focusing the physical and mental state of the learners in your group. It is also a useful tool for students to use in their own revision to help activate, energise and stimulate their brains.

> *'Recent brain research tells us that:*
> - *Physical stimulation boosts mental stimulation*
> - *Learning done with the body is generally more effective than with the mind only.*
> - *The engagement of emotions increases the impact and recall of learning experiences.'*

Eric Jensen, Brain-Based Learning. The Brain Store, Del Mar

> *'Research into kinesiology suggests that regular use of the Brain-Gym activities can alleviate stress, improve hand-eye co-ordination, improve the concentration on focused activities and quicken the response times to visual stimuli.'*

Alistair Smith, Accelerated Learning in the Classroom. Network Educational Press, Stafford

Some examples of Brain Gym® are described in Activity 4 in this workshop, but ideally should be interspersed throughout the revision course for full effect.

The bigger picture

The model of the brain offered here is a helpful initial tool for understanding how our brains operate and how they are able to learn. However, it is highly simplified and recent research has shown the brain's actual functioning to be far, far more complex than this model suggests.

Suggested reading:

Brain Compatible Classrooms	**Robin Fogarty**
Brain Based Learning	**Eric Jensen**
Accelerated Learning in Practice	**Alistair Smith**
Smart Moves	**Carla Hannaford**
(Chapter on Brain Gym®)	

'Your brain is like a sleeping giant.'

Tony Buzan
expert on the brain and learning

Workshop plan

Learning outcomes:

By the end of this workshop students will:
- be better acquainted with their brains
- know a number of strategies to make their revision more brain friendly
- know a range of Brain Gym® activities for use when revising.

Activity 1: Brain Facts – How well do you know your brain? (10 mins)

A warm-up exercise in which students are asked to decide if statements are true or false.

Activity 2: Building a living brain! (20 mins)

Students create a physical representation of the brain and its main structures. This exercise will hopefully help students to begin to understand the nature of this complex organ inside their heads.

Activity 3: Working *with* my brain (20 mins)

A matching activity where students match facts about the brain to revision/learning strategies and decide which strategies will be of use to them.

Activity 4: Brain Gym® (10 mins)

An introduction to Brain Gym® – showing students a range of activities to help 'wake up' their brains for revision.

Review: Two questions (10 mins)

1. What have we learned in this workshop?
2. How might this help us in our revision in the future?

The brain is wider than the sky

For put them side by side

The one the other will contain

With ease, and more beside.

Emily Dickinson
American poet

Activity 1: Brain Facts – How well do you know your brain?

Aim/s:	To begin to find out a little about our brains in an active way.
Resources:	None.

The activity

You could run this as a paper exercise, but it is much more fun, memorable and stimulating if done as a group exercise.

Ask students to sit in a circle and to stand up and change places if they agree with the statements listed below. After people have moved you can ask why people moved/didn't move and supply the correct answer (if there is one!). With a larger group this activity can be modified to become 'Stay standing if…'.

Stand up and change places if…

● **You think it's possible to carry on learning until you die**
True – yes, 'use it or lose it', just as you exercise to keep your body fit, you can keep learning as long as your brain is stimulated.

● **You think that bigger brains are better brains**
False – it's not the size of your brain that's important, it's how you use it that counts! Apparently Einstein had a relatively average-sized brain – we all have an amazing capacity to learn.

● **You think that colour and music can actually change the way your brain looks**
True – when stimulated with colour and music the appearance of the brain alters, with certain areas lighting up on brain scans. Try using lots of colour and experiment with playing certain types of music when you are revising – it might help you to make connections that will aid your recall.

● **You think that some people are just born 'brainier' than others**
False – although we don't fully understand the relationship, we do know that nurture (not nature) has a huge impact on our brainpower and how we learn – in fact some scientists believe you can learn how to be more intelligent.

● **You think brain is made up mostly of water**
True – and to function at its best the brain needs lots of water. Drink plenty of fresh water rather than tea, coffee or coke which actually de-hydrate the brain. If you feel thirsty you are already dehydrated.

' Brain functioning depends very much on what you've had for breakfast.'

Richard Restak

● **You think your brain likes chips and other fatty foods, sugary drinks, and cigarettes**

False – you may like these things, but as an organ your brain will be healthier and work better on a diet of fresh fruit, vegetables and protein. As for smoking, the brain uses 20 percent of the body's oxygen and people who smoke actually cut brain function by about 25 percent.

● **Brains can be exercised**

True – just as exercising will keep your body fit and well, there are exercises called Brain Gym® that will help wake up your brain and help the two hemispheres to work together effectively.

● **You think this exercise will help with your revision**

True – it should help you to know about your brain and how it works. It is also useful to be active when you're learning as you are helping to get more oxygen to your brain and you are more likely to remember learning in which you are actively involved.

‘I found out that learning is fun and interesting. ’

UFA student

'We can no longer short-change our brains and impoverish our spirits.'

Jean Houston
American educator & philosopher

Activity 2: Building a living brain!

> **Aim/s:** To use a physical approach through mime to construct a simple model of the brain and some of its functions in order to a nurture a sense of awe at this incredibly complex organ inside our heads.
>
> **Resources:** You will need some space for this activity and 6–14 volunteers.

The activity

You will need to ask for 6–14 volunteers who will, through mime, construct a simple model of the brain showing its different parts and their functions. In general the more the merrier.

Build the model up in stages, following the instructions below and then set the whole brain working together.

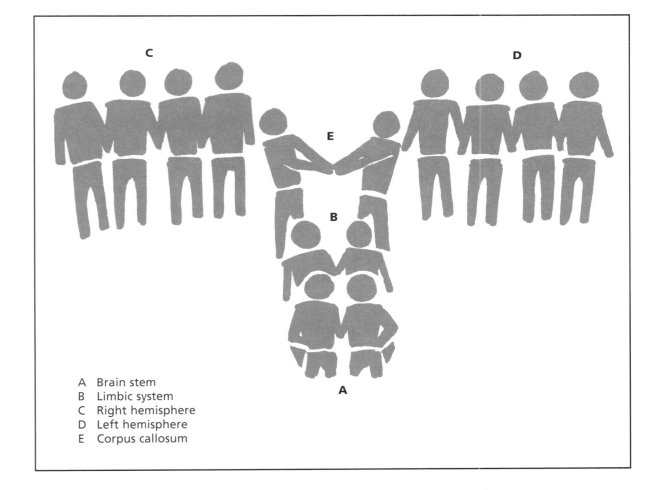

A Brain stem
B Limbic system
C Right hemisphere
D Left hemisphere
E Corpus callosum

'There is no more important responsibility in education than nurturing the pleasure of learning.'

Sheila Ostrander & Lyn Schroeder
experts on learning & psychic research

No. of people	Positioning	Role/function
👤 – 👥	Kneeling side by side facing front	**Brain stem (A)** This is the part that is formed from the nerves that come up from the spinal cord. In evolutionary terms it is probably the most primitive part of the brain and shares some aspects with present day reptiles! The brain stem regulates body functions such as breathing, heart rate, blood pressure – things over which we have no conscious control. This part of the brain is important for keeping us alive and governs our flight or fight response when we feel threatened. Suggested mimes: Taking pulse for heart rate; 'fight or flight'.
👤 – 👥	Kneeling behind brain stem	**Mid-brain/Limbic system (B)** A complex arrangement of modules, thought to be important for unconscious processing, more recently evolved than the brain stem. Structures in this area are important for processing memory and emotions. Suggested mime: one person mimes an emotion; one person mimes a memory.
👤 – 👥👥	Face front on right side	**Right hemisphere (C)** Important for/takes the lead in processing for: ● Music/rhythm ● Creativity ● Visual/spatial awareness ● Right hemisphere will deal with the 'whole'; sees the big picture Ask each volunteer to think of a mime for each of these functions.
👤 – 👥👥	Face front on left side	**Left hemisphere (D)** Important for/takes the lead in processing for: ● Language ● Logic ● Analysis/detail ● Left hemisphere will deal with the detail in a stimulus; perceives details/small steps Ask each volunteer to think of a mime for each of these functions.
👥	Standing at sides linking arms across top of mid-brain	**Corpus callosum (E)** This is a bundle of fibres (around 200 million!) connecting the left and right hemispheres. It sends electrical signals to and fro, ensuring the hemispheres work as a whole. Suggested mime: join hands and sway back and forth to show communication between left and right.

❝ As young teachers we ought to know more and more about the brain so we can help students to use their brainpower more fully – it really is amazing when you start to explore it and I want to do everything I can to build this into my teaching to help my students achieve. ❞

UFA tutor

'Go confidently
in the direction
of your
dreams!
Live the
life you've
imagined.'

Henry David Thoreau
American essayist & poet

Points to make

✔ Your brain is doing lots of things at the same time – many of which you're not even conscious of!

✔ Staying alive – keeping our heart going and keeping us safe is important and so parts of our brain will carry out those functions. It is possible that these functions take over and stop us from being able to carry out more complex tasks like problem solving/learning new things when we feel under stress.

✔ If we are worried, sad or angry we may not be able to think clearly.

✔ We need to make sure we are aware of the 'big picture' and the 'small steps' in any learning.

✔ The brain is able to process many stimuli at once – colour, music, sound etc. Perhaps we should try to make revision more multi-sensory?

Note

This activity is obviously simplified. Current research suggests the brain is much more complex than we think. Skills/functions are probably not only 'sited' in these areas mentioned below but are the result of many different parts of the brain working together. However, the best sort of learning (and revision) is likely to be multi-sensory, providing a rich range of stimuli for the brain to latch on to. For instance, why is it that we remember the words to songs effortlessly? How is it that advertising slogans stay with us for years, without us even trying to learn them? Perhaps by understanding a little more about how the brain functions we can build in some seemingly effortless approaches to revision?

Look after your brain

We all know that good athletes have to be fit. They have to eat well, sleep well and practise hard. They have to look after their bodies. To learn well you need to look after your brain.

You can improve brain power by:

- Getting plenty of sleep; this allows your theta and delta waves to buzz. Your brain needs time to sort out information that has come in during the day.

- Drinking lots of water – it helps to conduct electricity and speeds up learning by 30 percent. Dehydration will lead to headaches and tiredness. Water does not mean tea, coffee or coke... it means pure H_2O.

- Eating a balanced diet. Plenty of 'brain food' like fish and green vegetables really does help!

- Trying brain exercises helps to connect the right and left hemisphere for whole-brain learning.

- Exercise in general helps enormously; your brain uses up 20 percent of your total oxygen intake. Regular aerobic exercise is therefore very important. It also improves your mood and is helpful when you are stressed.

- Avoiding too much chocolate, coffee, sugar, coke, foods with E numbers and, of course, alcohol; these are bad for your brain. They interfere with the messages being passed from one cell to another.

Activity 3: Working *with* my brain

> **Aim/s:** To provide students with some practical strategies for their own revision. To show the usefulness of collaborative exercise and a more kinaesthetic approach to working with information.
>
> **Resources:** *Brain Facts & Revision Strategies* (one set per small group). These should be photocopied onto two different colours, cut up and placed in envelopes. The instructions for the activity can be stuck onto the envelopes.

The activity

1. Ask students to form groups of two to four and give each group an envelope containing Brain Facts and Revision Strategies. Now ask them to match up the facts to the strategies.

2. Once the groups have matched the cards, get them to look at the way other groups have completed the exercise to see if there is consensus.

3. Invite students to consider the following questions, first on their own and then ask them to share with a partner/rest of the group.

   - Which of these strategies do you think you can adopt right now?
   - Which do you think you might have a go at?
   - Do you have strategies of your own, that work for you, that fit with some of the brain facts?
   - Is there anything that you're going to stop doing?

Points to make

> ✔ The important thing to stress here is that different people learn in different ways and what works for one person will not necessarily work for others. However, a better understanding of the brain and how it works will help students revise in a more brain friendly way.

The full list of Brain Facts and their corresponding Revision Strategies appears below.

Brain Facts & Revision Strategies

F **Your brain can do many things at once. It can take in a range of different stimuli from lots of different sources. It is a parallel processor, using left and right sides of the brain at the same time.**

S Good revision uses both sides of the brain at once. Try to build lots of variety into your revision. Use as many different senses as you can and use music, movement and pictures as much as you can. Mind mapping (see Workshop Four) is especially good for this.

'The mind is not a vessel to be filled but a fire to be ignited.'

Plutarch
Greek historian & philospher

F Your brain processes parts and wholes at the same time. It likes to be aware of the big picture while focusing on the small steps it needs to take to get there.

S Make sure you know how the bits of your revision fit together. Figure out the big picture, then break it down into smaller bite-sized pieces that you need to learn.

F Your brain automatically focuses on what it knows, but at the same time will be searching for things that are new.

S Work from what you know, but also introduce new information – your brain is hungry for it!

F Emotions are really important. You won't learn much if you are stressed, angry, upset or tired. Your brain will learn best when you are feeling happy and enthusiastic.

S Try to be positive about your revision. Focus on what you have achieved rather than looking at things in a negative way. Talk to other people to get feedback on what you're doing. Try to find ways of getting yourself into a positive frame of mind. You can do it! Try relaxation techniques.

F Learning involves conscious and unconscious processing. Your brain needs 'down time' to sort through and make sense of what you've been revising.

S Give yourself regular breaks and time to reflect and think back over what you've done. Sleep is really important too – make sure you get enough sleep.

F The average concentration time is 20 minutes. After this your brain will not be as receptive.

S Have regular breaks – these need not be big breaks, but every 20 minutes or so make sure you stretch, do some Brain Gym® or think about something completely different.

F Your brain is the hungriest organ in the body, taking up 20 percent of the oxygen in your blood.

S Get plenty of exercise. A healthy mind needs physical exercise as well as mental stimulation. Get plenty of sleep.

F Thirst and hunger affect learning. The brain is made mostly of water.

S Eat sensibly, try to avoid lots of fatty foods and eat lots of fresh fruit and vegetables. Drink plenty of water. Try to avoid tea, coffee and coke as they have a high caffeine content that will dehydrate you.

F Your brain makes sense of information by making patterns and links between things.

S Try to find patterns in what you are learning. Use memory tricks like mnemonics and make up stories to remember things.

F Your brain will take on new information better in the morning.

S Use the morning to work on things that are new or things that you find hard. Use the afternoon to go over things you've already learned.

F Music can affect brain waves. Certain types of music are especially good for creating a state of relaxed alertness. The most effective is that which has 60–80 beats per minutes, which is very much like the beating of a human heart at rest.

S Try playing music when you are reviewing something you've already learnt. It helps absorption and storage of information. Music without lyrics with about 60–80 beats per minute is best.*

F Your brain will take in information from all around you, even if you're not concentrating on it.

S Display mind maps, diagrams, important facts etc. around the walls above eye level.

F Your brain needs to know why you're asking it to remember things – how is it relevant?

S Make sure you understand why you need to learn something – what's the reasoning behind it? Why is it important?

* See p. 242 for suggestions

 Brain Friendly Revision

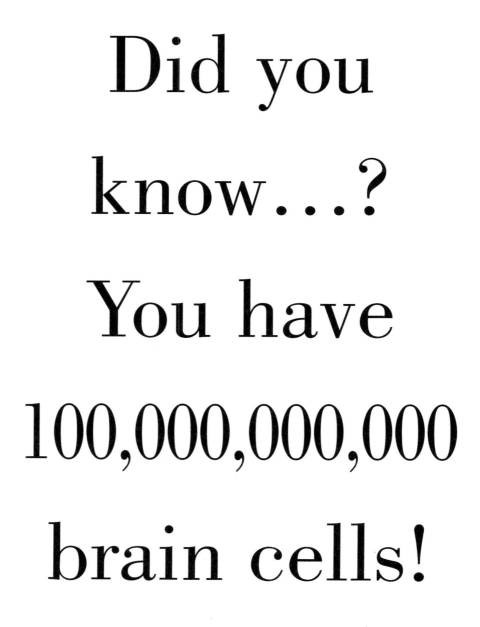

Did you know…? You have 100,000,000,000 brain cells!

Activity 4: Brain Gym® and other techniques

> **Aim/s:** This introduces students to a series of short snappy activities that may help to energise the brain and, used part way through a session, may help to refocus attention.
>
> **Resources:** Large sheets of paper. Felt pens (for Double Doodle).

The activity

Look at the following exercises and try out two to three with your group.

Nose/Ear Change

Hold your right ear with your left hand and then hold your nose with your right hand. Then switch so that you are holding your left ear with your right hand and your nose with your left hand. Try to speed up (without punching yourself!).

Cross Crawl

From standing, begin to march in time. As you raise your knees touch them with the opposite elbow.

Double Doodle

On a large sheet of paper, draw large, continuous and overlapping mirror shapes using both hands simultaneously. Using felt pens, continue to draw in easy looped movements. Begin with large simple shapes like circles, eights, squares or triangles. Be aware of the mirrored movements and graduate to more detailed drawing. This activity connects left and right brain and helps establish directionality and orientation in space. By exercising hand-eye co-ordination it will improve graphicacy and writing skills. It can be very relaxing.

Double Doodle Letters in the Air

With your preferred hand write out a letter – small case or capital. Practise different letters and then, using your other hand as well, write the mirror image of the letter. Next, try writing your whole name. If you are right-handed, start in the centre and work out. If you are left handed, start at the outside and work in. You could also do this with other keywords, formulae etc.

This can help to make difficult spellings memorable. Practice it with one hand to start off with and then both hands. Then on successful completion place the drawn image in your upper left field of vision and then try to write it with your eyes closed.

> 6 Amy found it very stimulating and enjoyable. 9
>
> Parent of UFA student

Some see things as they are and ask why?

I dream of things that never were and ask why not?

George Bernard Shaw
Irish dramatist

Lazy Eights

With one arm extended in front of you and your thumb pointed upwards, trace the shape of a figure eight in the air. The eight should be on its side and as you trace it out in large, slow movements focus your eyes on your thumb. Without moving your head, trace three eights in successively larger movements. Now do it with your other hand and then clasp them together and do both.

An alternative to this is to trace a 'lazy eight' with one hand. Then, with both hands starting in the centre, make yourself trace it in the opposite direction, so that if you start by tracing the eight with an upward movement with your right hand, you start the left hand with a downward movement.

Alphabet Edit

Alphabet Edit is a challenge. It is very useful for clearing the mind of any baggage brought into the classroom that might get in the way of learning. It involves saying the letters of the alphabet in sequence beginning to end (or end to beginning!) and completing actions to accompany specific letters. For example:

L = left arm raise
R = right arm raise
T = both arms together

It might help to write out the letters of the alphabet on the board or OHP and underneath each letter write an 'L', 'R' or 'T'. This way there is an action corresponding to each letter. Alternatively, just certain letters could have corresponding actions. Make up your own version – or ask students to suggest actions for some of the letters.

Points to make:

✔ Just as we exercise our bodies by a visit to the gym, we can also help to exercise our brains.

✔ Brain Gym® helps to activate and energise the brain by stimulating both sides of the brain and firing impulses across the corpus callosum.

✔ Use it at the beginning of a revision session to help get you focused or when you feel like you are becoming inattentive – remember the attention span of most adults is about 20 minutes.

✔ Research suggests that cross-body exercises such as Cross Crawl, Nose/Ear Change and Alphabet Edit improve co-ordination, visual, auditory and kinaesthetic ability and can improve listening, writing and memory.

'All human beings by nature, desire to know.'

Aristotle
Greek philosopher

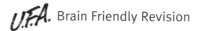

Brain Facts and Revision Strategies

The Brain Facts and the implications for revision need to be printed on two different colours and then cut up and placed in envelopes. The instructions for the activity can be stuck onto the envelope.

Instructions for activity

In this envelope you will find some 'Brain Facts'; you will also find some learning and teaching strategies.

1. Sort out the cards.
2. Look at the brain facts and think about which strategy is linked most closely to which brain fact.
3. There are also some blank cards – write down other helpful strategies that you use in your revision. Do they fit with any of the brain facts?

Instructions for activity

In this envelope you will find some 'Brain Facts'; you will also find some revision strategies.

1. Sort out the cards.
2. Look at the brain facts and think about which strategy is linked most closely to which brain fact.
3. There are also some blank cards – write down other helpful strategies that you use in your revision. Do they fit with any of the brain facts?

Brain Facts

Your brain can do many things at once. It can take in a range of different stimuli from lots of different sources. It is a parallel processor, using left and right sides of the brain at the same time.

Your brain processes parts and wholes at the same time. It likes to be aware of the big picture while focusing on the small steps it needs to take to get there.

Your brain automatically focuses on what it knows, but at the same time will be searching for things that are new.

Emotions are really important. You won't learn much if you are stressed, angry, upset or tired. Your brain will learn best when you are feeling happy and enthusiastic.

Learning involves conscious and unconscious processing. Your brain needs 'down time' to sort through and make sense of what you've been revising.

The average concentration time is 20 minutes. After this your brain will not be as receptive.

Your brain is the hungriest organ in the body, taking up 20 percent of the oxygen in your blood.

Thirst and hunger affect learning. The brain is made mostly of water.

Your brain makes sense of information by making patterns and links between things.

Your brain will take on new information better in the morning.

Music can affect brain waves. Certain types of music are especially good for creating a state of relaxed alertness. The most effective is that which has 60–80 beats per minute, which is very much like the beating of a human heart at rest.

Your brain will take in information from all around you, even if you're not concentrating on it.

Your brain needs to know why you're asking it to remember things – how is it relevant?

Revision Strategies

Good revision uses both sides of the brain at once. Try to build lots of variety into your revision. Use as many different senses as you can and use music, movement and pictures as much as you can. Mind mapping is especially good for this.

Make sure you know how the bits of your revision fit together. Figure out the big picture, then break it down into smaller bite-sized pieces that you need to learn.

Work from what you know, but also introduce new information – your brain is hungry for it!

Try to be positive about your revision. Focus on what you have achieved rather than looking at things in a negative way. Talk to other people to get feedback on what you're doing. Try to find ways of getting yourself into a positive frame of mind. You can do it! Try relaxation techniques.

Give yourself regular breaks and time to reflect and think back over what you've done. Sleep is really important too – make sure you get enough sleep.

Have regular breaks – these need not be big breaks, but every 20 minutes or so make sure you stretch, do some Brain Gym® or think about something completely different.

Get plenty of exercise. A healthy mind needs physical exercise as well as mental stimulation. Get plenty of sleep.

Eat sensibly, try to avoid lots of fatty foods and eat lots of fresh fruit and vegetables. Drink plenty of water. Try to avoid tea and coffee as they have a high caffeine content that will dehydrate you.

Try to find patterns in what you are learning. Use memory tricks like mnemonics and make up stories to remember things.

Use the morning to work on things that are new or things that you find hard. Use the afternoon to go over things you've already learned.

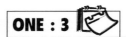

Try playing music when you are reviewing something you've already learnt. It helps absorption and storage of information. Music without lyrics and with about 60–80 beats per minute is best.

Display mind maps, diagrams, important facts etc. around the walls.

Make sure you understand why you need to learn something – what's the reasoning behind it? Why is it important?

WORKSHOP TWO

MY AMAZING INTELLIGENCE

'I realise that before I didn't really know my learning strengths, so I wasn't learning in a way that helped me — now I will.'

UFA student

My amazing intelligence

Many researchers have come to recognise that traditional measures of intelligence such as IQ are limiting and measuring up to this concept of intelligence makes many children feel like failures. According to Howard Gardner, intelligence should not be seen as a single, fixed, measurable phenomenon. Rather, his research has led him to take a much broader view of intelligence and he asserts that we have a range of eight intelligences, with each individual having a different intelligence profile. He stresses that we as educators should be concerned with harnessing the brain's natural potential for learning by fostering the whole range of these intelligences.

The implications of this for teachers are profound. No longer is intelligence seen as narrow, fixed and inherited. Instead we begin to see intelligence through a multifaceted filter and become aware of the learning potential within every child. The eight intelligence centres within the brain identified by Gardner – linguistic, mathematical/logical, kinaesthetic, visual/spatial, musical, naturalist, interpersonal and intrapersonal – provide the learner with a variety of ways of exploring and making sense of new information. The best learning will occur when as many of the intelligences as possible are both stimulated in new learning and also used to allow students to demonstrate or 'show what they know' in a variety of ways.

This more inclusive definition of intelligence fits well with brain based approaches to learning and allows greater numbers of young people to achieve.

The bigger picture

Gardner's theory is only one in an ever-increasing field looking into different models of intelligence. Many researchers have come to refute the notion of intelligence as measured by IQ tests. Emerging theories of intelligence focus more on what people can do and look to validate a much broader range of competencies. Goleman delineates five elements of what he calls Emotional Intelligence: self-awareness, self-regulation, motivation, empathy and social skill. Sternberg's theory of Successful Intelligence splits into three types of intelligence: analytical, creative and practical. Far from being in opposition to each other, these theories are in fact mutually reinforcing. They all argue for a view of intelligence that takes into account individual differences and recognises the impact that experience has on how we make sense of the world and how we make connections between things. Our challenge is to plan learning experiences that take into account these individual differences and to experiment with some of these theories of intelligence as models which can inform our planning.

Suggested reading:

Multiple Intelligences: The Theory in Practice   Howard Gardner

What matters is not how intelligent you are, but how you are intelligent.

Workshop plan

Learning outcomes:

By the end of the workshop students will:
- have explored the concept of intelligence, and specifically Howard Gardner's theory of Multiple Intelligences
- have a better understanding of their own intelligence strengths and how they can use these effectively in revision.

Activity 1: Intelligence Brainstorm (15 mins)

Students brainstorm the concept of intelligence. This may at first bring out the traditional view of intelligence, but further discussion will lead to a more practical definition of intelligence where a wider range of abilities is given status.

Activity 2: Multiple Intelligence questionnaire (15–20 minutes)

Students complete the 'How am I smart?' questionnaire to assess their intelligence profile.
The 'human bar graph' (see page 57) is one way of showing the range of intelligence strengths within a group.

Activity 3: Intelligence Jigsaw (10 minutes)

A matching activity to aid understanding of intelligence and what it means for approaches to revision.

Activity 4: One–Ten in Japanese (10 minutes)

Students explore how to use multiple intelligences practically in learning.

Review: Two questions (10 minutes)

1. What have we learned in this workshop?
2. How might this help us in our revision in the future?

Everyone

is

intelligent

Activity 1: Intelligence Brainstorm

15 mins

> **Aim/s:** To encourage students to see the range of words and phrases that are associated with intelligence and begin to verbalise their own thoughts about the concept of intelligence.
>
> **Resources:** Large sheets of paper. Pens.

The activity

Write the word 'intelligence' on the board and ask the students, in small groups, to 'free-associate' any words/phrases they can think of that are connected with the word intelligence and note them down. Make it clear at this stage that there are no right and wrong answers and all comments are valid.

After five minutes' discussion time ask for groups to feed back:

● words/phrases they think other groups will have thought of.

● words/phrases they think other groups will not have thought of.

Points to make:

✔ In the past people thought that intelligence was inherited and fixed – and people were either intelligent or not intelligent.

✔ More recent research suggests that there are different kinds of intelligence and that different people are intelligent in different ways. Everyone is intelligent.

✔ So, it is no longer about how intelligent you are, but *how* you are intelligent.

✔ The more intelligences you use the more brain power you use and the more effective your learning will be. The questionnaire we are going to do in the next activity will show you what your particular intelligence strengths are.

> ❝ My child finds schoolwork hard and is not very confident. It has been great for him and his self-esteem, which has enabled him to feel successful. ❞
>
> Parent of UFA student

The faster you admit to not having the answer to something, the more time you have to find one!

Activity 2: Multiple Intelligence questionnaire

> **Aim/s:** To provide a snapshot of people's intelligence strengths according to Howard Gardner's theory of Multiple Intelligences and to provoke discussion about different people's various strengths.
>
> **Resources:** *How am I smart? Multiple Intelligence questionnaire* (one per student). *Score sheet* (one per student). *Multiple Intelligence posters* (if possible, photocopy each onto a different coloured paper).

The activity

Hand out the questionnaires and ask students to fill them in as honestly as possible. They should try to go with their gut reaction and give the first answer that comes into their head. The questionnaire could be done individually or in pairs like an interview.

When the questionnaires have been completed ask students to calculate their scores using the score sheet.

Points to make:

✔ Everyone will have a different spread/profile of intelligences which may change over time.

✔ Howard Gardner says we should try to work to our strengths, but build on our weaknesses too. Trying to work with all the different intelligence strengths is best.

✔ All intelligences are equally good – a real super-learner tries to use as many as possible.

✔ The questionnaire is only a snapshot of someone's intelligence profile at any one time and so hard and fast conclusions should not be drawn from it. It is best used to provoke discussion about different people's different strengths.

Variations

It is possible to do the questionnaire in different ways according to the students' needs:

● Each student completes their own questionnaire (as above).

● Students read out the statements in groups but record their own scores for each statement.

● The tutor takes the whole group through the questionnaire, step by step.

'If we insist on looking at the rainbow of intelligence through a single filter, many minds will erroneously seem devoid of light.'

Renee Fuller
American psychologist

● A more kinaesthetic approach – arrange the questions by intelligence and create posters for each intelligence, displaying them at different 'intelligence stations' around the room. Students move around the stations recording their answers on an individual score sheet.

Human bar graph

You will need quite a lot of space for this.

Lay out the Multiple Intelligence posters side by side on the floor to make a horizontal axis. Now ask the students to queue up behind the poster which describes their predominant intelligence (the one they gave the highest score to). If they have equal top scores ask them to choose the one which they think describes them most accurately.

Points to make:

✔ In any group of people there will be a spread of different intelligences.

✔ Ask someone from each intelligence group to read out a description of the intelligence (see resources for Intelligence Jigsaw activity, pages 79–82).

✔ Look around at where people are – are they where you thought they would be? For example, are people who love PE standing in the kinaesthetic line, or people who like working in groups and talking things over in the interpersonal line? But also note that you are standing behind the intelligence poster for which you scored the highest. That is only part of the story – your intelligence profile is made up of this plus the seven other intelligences.

✔ Can this activity help you to think of new and interesting ways into some of your revision? Perhaps you can think of a musical way to revise maths, or a physical approach to history?

6 Overall, the UFA has given me an opportunity which has had a positive effect on me. It helped me to recognise the skills I had. 9

UFA student

'Nothing we ever imagined is beyond our powers, only beyond our present self-knowledge.'

Theodore Roszak
Professor of History & director of the
Ecopsychology Institute, California State University

Activity 3: Intelligence Jigsaw

Aim/s: Students consolidate their understanding of the different intelligences and think a bit more about how they can use them.

Resources: *Intelligence labels. Intelligence descriptions. Intelligence pictures. (One set of each per group.)*

The activity

Divide the students into small groups and give each group a copy of the intelligence pictures, the intelligence labels and the descriptions of different intelligence strengths. Ask the students to match the label, picture and description for each of the eight intelligences. Ask them also to be thinking about their own revision habits and the new things they might try out.

Feedback/discussion

Finish with a very short feedback session to ensure that the groups have made the correct matches. Also ask if anyone has had any ideas for new approaches to their revision – things they would like to try out.

Points to make:

✔ Revision is not just about sitting and looking through the notes you made in class.

✔ Looking at Gardner's theory of Multiple Intelligences we now know that different people learn in different ways.

✔ To make revision more exciting, more effective and much more fun we can try different ways of revising.

✔ If you are able to revise the same subject matter in a number of different ways, your understanding of it will be much deeper and you will be more likely to remember it for longer.

❛ Children are able to see that they are intelligent. ❜

UFA tutor

If you do what you've always done, you'll get what you've always got.

Old adage

Activity 4: One–ten in Japanese (in only four minutes!)

> **Aim/s:** To show how much easier it is to learn something by using more intelligences and more of your brain power.
>
> **Resources:** You will need quite a lot of space for this activity – the more the students can move around copying your mimes the better.

The activity

1. Explain to the students that, in only four minutes, they will be able to count to ten in Japanese. Now ask them just to watch you and listen to the following story.

Imagine a family day out at the seaside – everyone's there having a great time, it's a lovely sunny day.

Story	Japanese	Mime
I was playing around on the beach and I had a very itchy knee...	**(itchi = 1, ni = 2)**	**(scratch knee)**
So I bent down and rubbed it in the san'...	**(san = 3)**	**(rub knee in sand)**
When I looked up I saw a girl, she was playing at the other end of the beach...	**(shi = 4)**	**(Point to girl)**
I decided to go and see what she was up to...	**(go = 5)**	**(point to distance)**
I walked all the way to the other end of the beach where there was a huge rock-u...	**(roku = 6)**	**(walk and show outline shape of rock with hands)**
From behind the rocku came the sound of someone sneezing – shi-chi!...	**(shi-chi = 7)**	**(sneeze making the shi-chi sound)**
I went to see who had sneezed and standing with her back to me there was a woman wearing a huge hat-she turned round...	**(hachi = 8)**	**(get someone to be the woman and mime huge hat)**
She told me she was in a queue...	**(kyu = 9)**	**(make a line with several others)**
For a boat trip that was due...	**(ju = 10)**	**(look at watch)**

> ❛My son really enjoyed himself and had fun.❜
>
> Parent of UFA student

Everyone can become more intelligent.

2. Next ask the students to do the story with you with all the actions.

3. Ask the students to do the actions and not the words.

4. Now ask them to do the words but not the actions.

Points to make

After the students have done these last two parts of the activity ask them what was happening:

✔ When they just did the actions – many of them may have been sub-vocalising the words or could hear the words in their heads.

✔ When they just said the words – many of them may have been 'twitching' because they wanted to do the actions or were feeling the actions in their body, or were imagining doing the actions in their mind's eye even though they weren't actually doing the actions.

Perhaps the reason this happens is because they have stimulated a number of different intelligence centres through the way in which they learned the numbers. The brain hooks these centres in to help remember.

Feedback/discussion

Which intelligences did we use?
Mostly: linguistic, visual/spatial and kinaesthetic, but also: logical/mathematical; interpersonal?

It's about realising that you can use lots of techniques, trying to tap into kids and help them see that they can do it.

UFA tutor

'Attitudes are contagious. Are yours worth catching?'

Anon.

How am I smart?
Multiple Intelligence questionnaire

We all learn in different ways and this questionnaire is designed to give you a chance to work out how you learn best. Please read each question and then think how far this describes you. Circle a number 0,1,2,3,4 or 5 depending on whether it describes you very well (5) or not at all (0) or somewhere in middle (1,2,3 or 4). Take time to do it. Do it with your friends or alone – it's up to you.

Remember, this is for you – it will help you understand how you learn best, so… be as honest as you can!

1.	I always do things step by step and bit by bit.	0	1	2	3	4	5
2.	I know a lot about birds, animals and plants. I can recognise and name them.	0	1	2	3	4	5
3.	I enjoy taking notes and I am good at it.	0	1	2	3	4	5
4.	I like to learn by listening to other people.	0	1	2	3	4	5
5.	I like to get my hands on learning. I like to make things or use real objects when I learn.	0	1	2	3	4	5
6.	I watch carefully and often see things that other people miss.	0	1	2	3	4	5
7.	When I have to work something out, I like to ask questions and talk about it.	0	1	2	3	4	5
8.	I remember things like phone numbers by repeating them over and over.	0	1	2	3	4	5

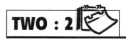

9. I like to use charts and diagrams and pictures to help me learn.

0 1 2 3 4 5

10. I can sense when people around me are in a good or bad mood.

0 1 2 3 4 5

11. I like to be outside rather than inside.

0 1 2 3 4 5

12. I learn best when I have to get up and do it for myself.

0 1 2 3 4 5

13. When I have a lot to do I make a list and use it to help me.

0 1 2 3 4 5

14. I need to know what the point of learning something is before I can feel interested.

0 1 2 3 4 5

15. I find it easier to work something out when I am walking or running.

0 1 2 3 4 5

16. I can explain things to people and help them to understand.

0 1 2 3 4 5

17. If I am in a new place I am good at finding places.

0 1 2 3 4 5

18. I can sort out arguments between friends.

0 1 2 3 4 5

19. I can remember words to music easily.

0 1 2 3 4 5

20. I can take things apart and put them together again easily.

0 1 2 3 4 5

21. I like taking part in games that involve other people.

0 1 2 3 4 5

22. I like to be quiet when I am working and thinking.   0 1 2 3 4 5

23. When I listen to music I can pick out individual instruments.   0 1 2 3 4 5

24. When I look at something, either a picture or something written, I can see patterns easily.   0 1 2 3 4 5

25. I am a good team player. I listen to other people and use their ideas.   0 1 2 3 4 5

26. I am interested in why people do what they do, I am interested in how other people behave.   0 1 2 3 4 5

27. I get restless easily, I fidget, I don't like to be still.   0 1 2 3 4 5

28. I like to work on my own.   0 1 2 3 4 5

29. I like to make music.   0 1 2 3 4 5

30. I get angry when I see pollution or the planet being harmed in any way.   0 1 2 3 4 5

31. I like to play with numbers – they interest me.   0 1 2 3 4 5

32. I think for myself. I know my own mind well.   0 1 2 3 4 5

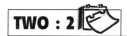

Score sheet

When you have done this, work with a friend to add up your scores.

1. Look back to each statement and see what score you gave yourself for that statement.
2. Fill in your score.
3. Add up your total for each intelligence.

Type of learner	Statements				Total
Interpersonal	**10**	**18**	**21**	**25**	
My score	—	—	—	—	_____
Intrapersonal	**14**	**22**	**28**	**32**	
My score	—	—	—	—	_____
Linguistic	**3**	**4**	**7**	**16**	
My score	—	—	—	—	_____
Mathematical/Logical	**1**	**13**	**24**	**31**	
My score	—	—	—	—	_____
Visual/Spatial	**6**	**9**	**17**	**20**	
My score	—	—	—	—	_____
Musical	**8**	**19**	**23**	**29**	
My score	—	—	—	—	_____
Naturalistic	**2**	**11**	**26**	**30**	
My score	—	—	—	—	_____
Kinaesthetic	**5**	**12**	**15**	**27**	
My score	—	—	—	—	_____

What does your intelligence pattern look like?

U.F.A. Brain Friendly Revision

Multiple Intelligences

INTERPERSONAL

 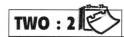

Multiple Intelligences

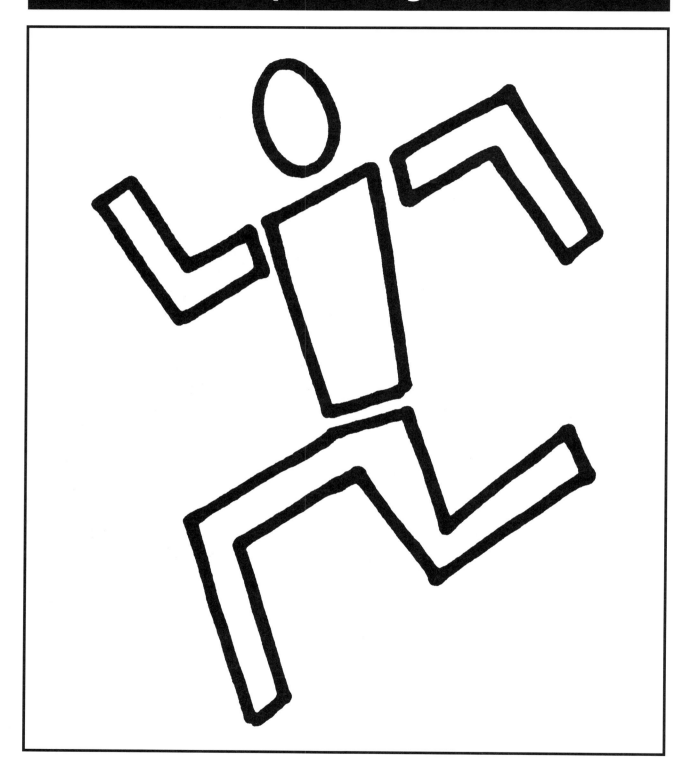

KINAESTHETIC

Multiple Intelligences

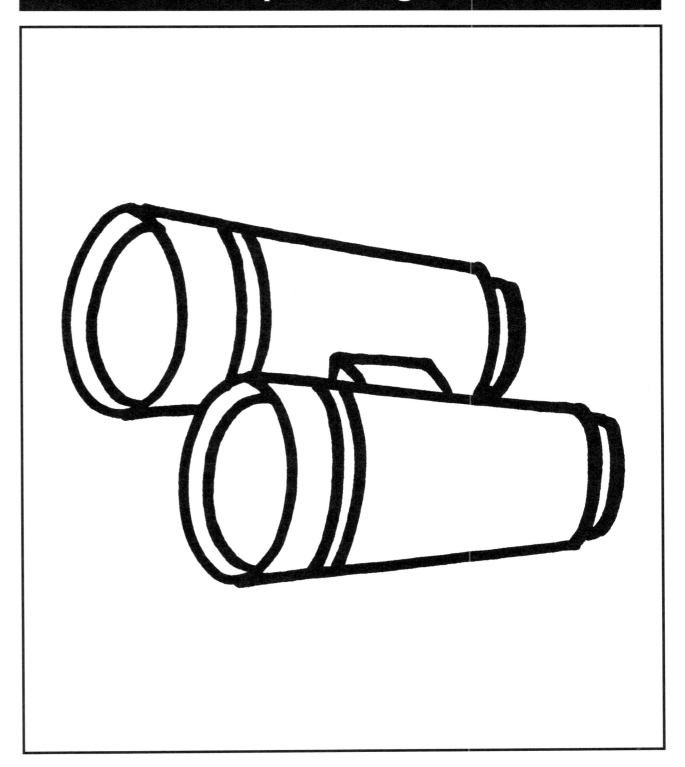

VISUAL/SPATIAL

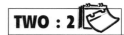

Multiple Intelligences

NATURALISTIC

U.F.A. Brain Friendly Revision

Multiple Intelligences

MUSICAL

Multiple Intelligences

LINGUISTIC

U.F.A. Brain Friendly Revision

 TWO : 2

Multiple Intelligences

MATHEMATICAL/LOGICAL

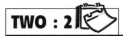

Multiple Intelligences

INTRAPERSONAL

U.F.A. Brain Friendly Revision

Intelligence Jigsaw – labels

Match the following intelligence labels to the pictures and descriptions.

INTERPERSONAL

INTRAPERSONAL

MUSICAL

KINAESTHETIC (PHYSICAL)

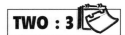
VISUAL/SPATIAL

MATHEMATICAL/ LOGICAL

LINGUISTIC

NATURALISTIC

U.F.A. Brain Friendly Revision

Intelligence Jigsaw – descriptions

- ● I can hear patterns in sound and I enjoy working with sounds. I am sensitive to sounds around me.

- ● Music sometimes makes me feel emotional.

- ● I enjoy improvising and playing with sound.

- ● I revise well with music in the background.

- ● I enjoy learning when rhythm and sound are part of the activity.

- ● Making up rhythmic chants and songs about things I need to remember will help me revise.

- ▲ I can see things from someone else's point of view easily.

- ▲ I find it easy to get on well with a range of different people.

- ▲ I enjoy working in groups.

- ▲ I learn best when I can share my learning with others.

- ▲ I enjoy revising with other people and find it useful to test out what I know with others.

◆ I have a strong sense of fairness and quickly see when something is unfair.

◆ I can describe features of the natural environment and can see patterns within and between living things.

◆ I am concerned about the effect the human race is having on the environment.

◆ I am particularly interested in environmental issues.

◆ I enjoy working outdoors and I learn well outdoors.

◆ Sometimes I take a walk to allow my learning to sink in.

▼ I enjoy using symbols and codes for things.

▼ I enjoy and am good at solving logical puzzles and working out sequences.

▼ I am able to see patterns between things easily.

▼ I like to learn in an ordered way and learn by doing things step by step.

▼ Making a clear revision timetable will help me to plan to cover everything.

■ I enjoy playing with language.

■ I often want to write things down.

■ I can listen for long periods of time.

■ I like to talk out loud to myself if I am trying to learn something.

■ I learn best by listening, writing, reading and discussion.

■ Creating stories around what I need to learn will help me to revise.

✦ I am very aware of my own feelings about lots of things.

✦ I think a lot.

✦ I have strong personal beliefs and values.

✦ I enjoy time on my own to think things through.

✦ I learn best when I am given time on my own to reflect on what I've been learning.

✦ Being aware of my thought processes as I remember helps me to revise.

✚ I am able to picture things in my head easily.

✚ I am able to move my body and objects through space easily.

✚ I am able to plan and build 3-dimensional objects.

✚ I like to learn by looking and observing.

✚ I enjoy revising from graphs, diagrams, pictures and mind maps. I love using colour.

∎ I love to explore things through touch and movement.

∎ I enjoy field trips, drama and model building.

∎ I have good co-ordination and sense of timing.

∎ I sometimes feel restless in a classroom.

∎ I revise best by doing.

∎ Planning regular stretch breaks/exercise helps me to revise more effectively.

∎ Creating mimes/actions helps me to remember key points.

Intelligences pictures

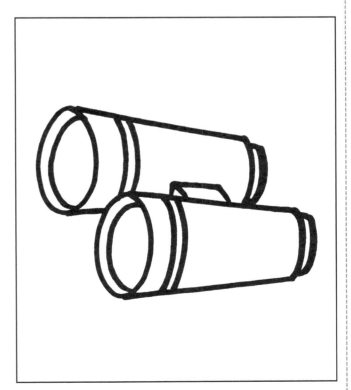

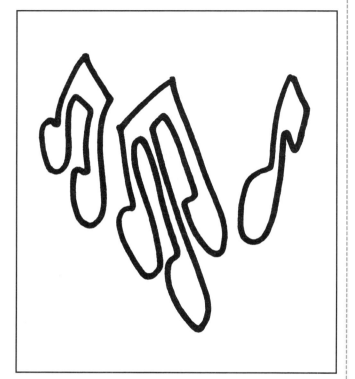

WORKSHOP THREE

GETTING READY TO REVISE

'As a result of today I am going to try to have more confidence in myself and be proud of my abilities and myself at all times.'

UFA student

Getting ready to revise

Helping students to become more aware of what drives them is going to empower them to take control of their learning. It is easy with revision to fall into a cycle of poor work habits, which produce limited success, making the student feel that they were just not born able enough to succeed in the way they want. This lack of self-belief becomes limiting, making revision or learning a laborious task that has to be endured. Visioning success and working in a brain friendly way optimises the learning and we know that success breeds success. Helping students understand that they can accelerate their learning by making some simple changes to their work habits is vital. We want them to work smarter, not harder.

Recent research into the brain has shown that what we put into our bodies affects how effectively our brain operates. A good diet, adequate sleep and plenty of water helps the learning to happen at the most basic chemical level. It is important that choices about what we put into our bodies are made knowing the consequences, good or bad.

Stress is the enemy of learning and helping students to be in control of their revision programme will reduce the likelihood of students stepping onto a downward spiral with their revision.

The bigger picture

The activities included here are by no means exhaustive. You may wish to build topics such as time management, finding out what you need to know and making a revision timetable into the work you do with students in this area. This workshop serves as a starting point and can be supplemented by a range of study skills and exam technique activities.

Suggested reading:

Accelerated Learning in Practice   **Alistair Smith**

'Whatever you can do or dream you can, begin it. Boldness has genius power and magic in it. Begin it now!'

Goethe
German poet & dramatist

Workshop plan

Learning outcomes:

By the end of the workshops students will:
- have a greater awareness of their current individual revision habits
- have developed an understanding of the need to have a positive mindset and they will have explored some simple techniques for doing this
- have tried out a relaxation exercise that can be used to combat stress
- have identified some barriers to successful revision and ways to overcome these.

Activity 1: What are my revision habits? (20 minutes)

In this activity the students complete two worksheets. Initially this is done individually with some time at the end to compare their findings with others.

This activity allows the students to reflect on what motivates them to learn and what their current revision habits are. This will allow them to identify areas which need to be changed to make their revision more effective.

Activity 2: Asking positive questions (20–25 minutes)

This activity begins to explore simple ways to turn negative thoughts into positive ones so that mental barriers to learning are overcome. It begins with a whole-group discussion on negative questions that students get trapped into asking and ends with the students themselves exploring how negative questions can be turned into more productive questions.

Activity 3: Barriers to revision (20–30 minutes)

This is a group activity where students brainstorm potential barriers to effective revision and ways to overcome these. Their ideas are collected at the end in a whole-group discussion.

After the discussion, the paired role-play gives students the chance to articulate ways of improving their revision.

Activity 4: Planning for effective revision (30–40 minutes)

This activity outlines some of the elements for planning effective revision and encourages students to think about key actions and when they are needed, as well as reinforcing effective revision habits.

Review: Traffic lights (10 minutes)

Using traffic lights as a metaphor, students are asked to decide on things they are going to start doing as a result of the session (green), things they are going to continue to do (amber) and things they are going to stop doing (red).

Every single individual is capable of achieving success!

Activity 1: What are my revision habits?

> **Aim/s:** To help students recognise what motivates and de-motivates them, and to identify areas where they could improve their work habits and make their revision more effective.
>
> **Resources:** *What motivates – what de-motivates? It's up to you* (one per student). *Revision – getting started* (one per student).

The activity

1. As a whole class, begin by discussing:
   - What is revision?
   - Why revise?
   - How many people enjoy revising?
   - How do you know you are doing it right?

2. Hand out the sheet 'What motivates – what de-motivates? It's up to you' and ask the students to circle any that apply to them.

☹ **Possible de-motivators:**	☺ **Possible motivators:**
✗ Not understanding the work	✓ Praise and reward
✗ Feeling ignored	✓ Good marks
✗ Criticism	✓ Being able to see steady improvement
✗ Frustration with studying – feeling you are not getting anywhere	✓ Setting and achieving targets
✗ Poor marks	✓ Understanding your work
✗ Low confidence	✓ When someone says 'think'!
✗ Too much pressure to do well	✓ Being told you are capable of achieving
✗ Very little praise	
✗ Slow or little progress	✓ People who believe in you
✗ Being late with work and feeling like you will never catch up	✓ Enjoying the subject

3. Now invite the students to move around the room and find someone who has circled at least two of the same phrases in either the top or the bottom box. When they have done this they should ask them a) how they deal with the de-motivators and b) how they make motivating things happen more often. Ask students to make some notes on the sheet about the discussion they've had or thoughts that have occurred to them.

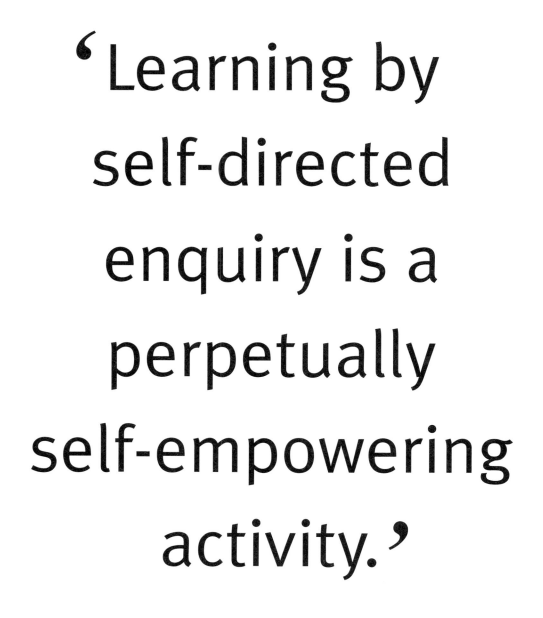

'Learning by self-directed enquiry is a perpetually self-empowering activity.'

Charles D. Hayes
American philosopher & publisher

4. Ask students to use the sheet 'Revision - getting started' to reflect on work habits. Ask them to fill in the questionnaire individually, being as honest as they can. It is designed to give them a chance to think about their own strengths and weaknesses so that they can get the most benefit out of the sessions.

5. After the scores have been calculated, ask students to look at their questionnaire and think about which statements they need to work on to 'move up' one box , e.g. from 'Not like me at all' to 'Like me sometimes'. They should ask themselves:
    ● Which areas do I need to work on?
    ● How do I need to change my revision habits?

Points to make:

✔ In order for us to do well, we need to know what motivates us. Top-class athletes know how to motivate themselves to train in order to be the best in their sport. Understanding what motivates you will help you with your revision – try to build on these strategies. Also, knowing what de-motivates will help – try to minimise these.

✔ It is important to be in the right frame of mind for revision – know why you're doing it and what you need to do.

❝ I thought by mid-week he would be bored, but this was not the case. In fact, as the week wore on, he was more impressed with each day's task. ❞

Parent of UFA student

The limits to learning are mostly self-imposed.

Activity 2: Asking positive questions

Aim/s: To explore ways of turning negative thoughts into positive ones in order to help to overcome psychological barriers to learning.
Resources: None.

20-25 mins

The activity

1. As a whole group, invite discussion on the following:
    ● How important is what you believe about yourself?
    ● Can you think of examples in your past experience when strong beliefs (negative or positive) have influenced the outcome of events?

2. Brainstorm on the board some negative questions students often ask in learning situations.
    What 'secret' messages are you giving to your brain? How can these be turned into positive questions?

Examples:

Dead-end question	– Why does this teacher always give me hours of homework?
Positive question	– How can I get this homework done?
Dead-end question	– Why do we have to do boring work?
Positive question	– How can I make the work more interesting?
Dead-end question	– How come this teacher gave me a lower grade than I deserved?
Positive question	– (ask for suggestions)
Dead-end question	– Why does this teacher always pick on me?
Positive question	– (ask for suggestions)

3. Ask the students to:
    ● think individually, of five dead-end questions they might ask about their revision
    ● write them down and then write down how they feel having asked them
    ● work in pairs to write the positive versions of the questions.

Now how do they feel?

Points to make:

✔ Emphasise the importance of self-belief in achieving your aims and how mindset can influence your learning. If you feel good about learning you will have more success with it. Positive thinking is important. Negative mindsets put up barriers that stop learning.

❝ It really helped in raising self-esteem and confidence. ❞
Parent of UFA student

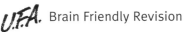

Dream it...

Do it!

Activity 3: Overcoming barriers to learning

> **Aim/s:** For students to explore potential barriers to revision and how to overcome them.
> **Resources:** Large sheets of paper and pens for group brainstorm.

20–30 mins

The activity

1. Ask students to work in groups of three or four and ask each group to brainstorm things that they think stop them from revising or learning effectively.

2. Now ask the groups to decide on two of the barriers they have come up with (one they think everyone will have identified and one they think nobody else will have identified) and concentrate their discussion on finding ways of overcoming these barriers. They will need to make a note of these.

3. Ask each group to feed back a summary of their discussion to the whole group.

   Some barriers that may get identified:

   ✖ Poor organisation ✖ Not knowing how to revise
   ✖ Confusing notes to revise from ✖ Leaving it too late
   ✖ Nowhere to revise ✖ Bad memory
   ✖ Thinking you can't do it ✖ Hating revising
   ✖ Parents/other people ✖ Not enough time
   ✖ Cramming ✖ Other things to do
   ✖ Too much to revise

Points to make:

✔ During the feedback discussion it is important to emphasise that there are many simple ways to minimise the barriers to effective learning. By doing so they will make their revision more enjoyable and more successful.

Follow up

In pairs, students role-play the following:

The revision clinic: One person plays the lousy learner who goes into the clinic to get help with their revision problems. The other person plays the super-learner who listens sympathetically to the problems the lousy learner has and offers helpful advice on how to overcome the problems. After each problem, the students swap roles. At the end, sum up – what have we learnt from this?

'I really enjoyed the challenge.'

UFA student

 Brain Friendly Revision

Sleep is important too!

Relax before you go to sleep. You need around 8 hours' sleep time.

Theta brain waves are those which occur during 'dream time' or Rapid Eye Movement time when you are asleep, thought to be about 20 percent of your total sleep time. Your brain uses this time to sort out information that has come in during the day and file it away. You are subconsciously problem solving or discovering answers to puzzling or difficult questions. You will tend to remember information that you have scanned or listened to on tape just before going to sleep.

Try it!

Make sure you have enough sleep and allow this sorting out to happen.

Activity 4: Planning for effective revision

> **Aim/s:** For students to begin to think about key organisational tasks and good revision habits which will help them plan their revision programme effectively.
>
> **Resources:** *Planning for effective revision – statements*. This activity will need to be prepared in advance. The statements need to be photocopied onto paper of two different colours, cut up and placed in envelopes, one for each group. Laminating will allow you to use this activity over and over again.

The activity

Pupils should work in groups of four. Give each group an envelope which contains the 'Planning for effective revision' statements and allow five minutes for them to read through each of the statements and just familiarise themselves with the range.

Rules of the activity:

1. There are five stages to the activity and a different person has to be the spokesperson for the group in the first four stages. Remember, the spokesperson is speaking for the group and not just themselves.

2. Each stage will be two-three minutes long, giving the group time to make their decision and be able to justify it. Stage five may need to be a little longer.

3. We must stick to the time limits.

    Stage one: Sort the statements into two piles; one of things you only have to do once or twice and the other of things you have to do all the time.

    Stage two: Choose two statements that are easy to do.

    Stage three: Choose two statements that you think are the most important for success with revision.

    Stage four: Choose two statements that you think are the least important.

    Stage five: Put all the statements in order beginning with the one you would do first.

At the end of the first four rounds take feedback from each group. They should feedback **WHAT** they have decided and **WHY**. Stress that there are no definite right and wrong answers and that the purpose is to explore our opinions.

At the end of stage five ask students to walk around and look at the way in which the other groups have ordered their statements.

> ‘As a result of today I'm going to:
> Make a timetable!
> Do revision! ’
>
> UFA student

Can music help me to learn?

YES!

Research show that certain types of music can really help you to learn. Play low volume, non-lyrical (no words) classical music (60 beats per minute)* when you are studying and concentrating. It cuts out distracting background noise and increases your subconscious alpha waves, which help you to learn faster.

* See p.242

U.F.A. Brain Friendly Revision

Follow-on

A way of consolidating and personalising this activity is to give students time to make their own flow diagram using the statements to help them to plan what they are going to do and in what order. Encourage students to add realistic times and dates to each stage of their diagram. This will help to make it happen. Those statements relating to things that need doing all the time can be added around the edges.

Statements:

⇨ Make a list of all the subjects you are revising for. For each subject make a list of the important topics you need to cover.

⇨ Look through the syllabus/check with your teacher and make sure that you have covered each topic that may come up.

⇨ Make a detailed revision timetable several weeks before the exam. Decide what you will be studying and when. Make sure you have included time-out to relax and do other things.

⇨ Find out how many papers there are for each subject. Find out where, when and how long each exam is. Do you know what each paper will cover?

⇨ Organise a place to work. Try to clear the space of distractions. Decide how to organise your space for how you like to work – what do you need? A chair and desk are useful – you need to be comfortable and have enough light. If you can, clear some space on the walls to put up posters, mind maps, reminders etc.

⇨ Collect together any resources you might need such as coloured pens/pencils, paper, post-it notes, a tape recorder, textbooks, library books etc.

⇨ Do a 'reality check' – check your understanding of what you have been revising.

⇨ Decide how much time you need to spend on each area.

⇨ Take regular 'stretch breaks'. Every 20 minutes or so move about, stretch and then re-focus.

⇨ Keep your revision organised – know exactly where you are with things. If your timetable slips, re-organise it realistically so you can still cover everything.

⇨ Figure out what you already know.

⇨ Review your notes on the same day as you make them. This helps you to remember them because the topic is fresh in your mind.

⇨ Get into the right state of mind, think positively and believe in yourself. Remember, 'Whether you think you can or you think you can't, you're probably right'.

⇨ Think about why you want to succeed – what are your hopes for the future?

'Quality isn't about not making mistakes; it's about not making the same mistakes twice.'

Clair Eberhart
custom builder in Boise, Idaho

⇨ Drink water, eat high-energy foods and get enough sleep. Your brain needs to be rested and fed and watered properly if it is to learn effectively.

⇨ Get plenty of exercise – your brain needs it!

⇨ Make a note of how you spend your time during an average day. Look back over the day and figure out how you could use your time more effectively. Decide what's important and what's not.

⇨ Share your goals with someone else – it will help you to achieve them.

⇨ Review what you have revised after ten minutes, at the end of the day, within 48 hours, weekly and monthly.

⇨ Use lots of different ways of studying each time you study: mind maps, pictures, body actions, taping your notes and using flash cards are just some.

6 There were goals she could achieve and prove to herself, which means a lot. 9

Parent of UFA student

'Many of life's failures are people who did not realise how close they were when they gave up.'

Thomas Edison
American inventor

What motivates – what de-motivates? It's up to you

Do any of these turn you *off* learning?

Circle those that apply to you (add any of your own that are not here).

☹ Not understanding the work

☹ Feeling ignored

☹ Criticism

☹ Poor marks

☹ Low confidence

☹ Frustration with studying - feeling you are not getting anywhere

☹ Very little praise

☹ Too much pressure to do well

☹ Slow or little progress

☹ Being late with work and feeling that you will never catch up

Do any of these turn you *on* to learning?

Circle those that apply to you (add any of your own that are not here).

☺ Praise and reward

☺ Good marks

☺ Being able to see steady improvement

☺ Setting and achieving targets

☺ Understanding your work

☺ When someone says 'think!'

☺ Being told you are capable of achieving

☺ People who believe in you

☺ Enjoying the subject

Now move around the room and find someone who has circled at least two the same as you in either the top or bottom box.

Look at the one you've circled in the top box – ask the person:
'How do you deal with this?'

Look at the one you've circled in the bottom box – ask the person:
'How do you make this happen more of the time?'

Think about how many ways people have of minimising the de-motivators (things that put you off learning) and maximising the motivators.

My notes:

Revision – getting started

To help you get the most out of this revision programme you need to think about yourself as a learner. This questionnaire is only going to be seen by you and so it is important to be as honest as you can.

It is designed to give you a chance to think about your own learning strengths and weaknesses so that you can get the most benefit out of the sessions.

My strengths and weaknesses

	Just like me	Like me some-times	Not like me at all
1. I know how to make myself work, even when I don't want to.			
2. I organise my day, my work and my free time so that I can meet deadlines.			
3. I plan each revision session and review my progress at the end.			
4. I make easy-to-remember notes, using keywords and ideas only.			
5. I know why I am studying and how it will help me in later life.			
6. I know what my own learning style is and I use it to help my revision.			
7. I often draw colourful charts and pictures to help me learn.			
8. I regularly ask questions about what I'm learning.			
9. I see school as a stepping stone to success in life.			
10. I believe in myself, think positively and remain confident even when things go wrong for me.			
11. I worry about revision and exams.			
12. I revise in a tidy, organised workspace.			
13. I make a revision timetable at least eight weeks before the exams.			
14. I stick to my revision timetable.			
15. I enjoy learning.			

Your score

Count up the ticks. Which column has the most ticks?

Mostly 'Just like me'
This is brilliant. You certainly are a super-learner! By discovering a few more techniques you could be better still!

Mostly 'Sometimes like me'
You have lots of good ways to learn already. By learning a few more, you can improve your ability to revise and pass exams.

Mostly 'Not like me at all'
Now is the time to begin to learn how to learn. Remember, everyone can learn and learning can be fun and enjoyable. We are all intelligent.

Planning for effective revision – statements

Make a list of all the subjects you are revising for. For each subject make a list of the important topics you need to cover.

Look through the syllabus/check with your teacher and make sure that you have covered each topic that may come up.

Make a detailed revision timetable several weeks before the exam. Decide what you will be studying and when. Make sure you have included time-out to relax and do other things.

Find out how many papers there are for each subject. Find out where, when and how long each exam is. Do you know what each paper will cover?

Figure out what you already know.

Organise a place to work. Try to clear the space of distractions. Decide how to organise your space for how you like to work – what do you need? A chair and desk are useful. You need to be comfortable and have enough light. If you can, clear some space on the walls to put up posters, mind maps, reminders etc.

Collect together any resources you might need such as coloured pens/pencils, paper, post-it notes, a tape recorder, textbooks, library books etc.

Do a 'reality check' – check your understanding of what you have been revising.

Decide how much time you need to spend on each area.

Take regular 'stretch breaks'. Every 20 minutes or so move about, stretch and then re-focus.

U.F.A. Brain Friendly Revision

Keep your revision organised – know exactly where you are with things. If your timetable slips, re-organise it realistically so you can still cover everything.

Review your notes on the same day as you make them. This helps you to remember them because the topic is fresh in your mind.

Get into the right state of mind, think positively and believe in yourself. Remember, 'Whether you think you can or you think you can't, you're probably right'.

Think about why you want to succeed – what are your hopes for the future?

Drink water, eat high-energy foods and get enough sleep. Your brain needs to be rested and fed and watered properly if it is to learn effectively.

Get plenty of exercise – your brain needs it!

Make a note of how you spend your time during an average day. Look back over the day and figure out how you could use your time more effectively. Decide what's important and what's not.

Share your goals with someone else – that will help you to achieve them.

Review what you have revised after 10 minutes, at the end of the day, within 48 hours, weekly and monthly.

Use lots of different ways of studying each time you study: mind maps, pictures, body actions, taping your notes and using flash cards are just some.

U.F.A. Brain Friendly Revision

WORKSHOP FOUR

MIND MAPPING

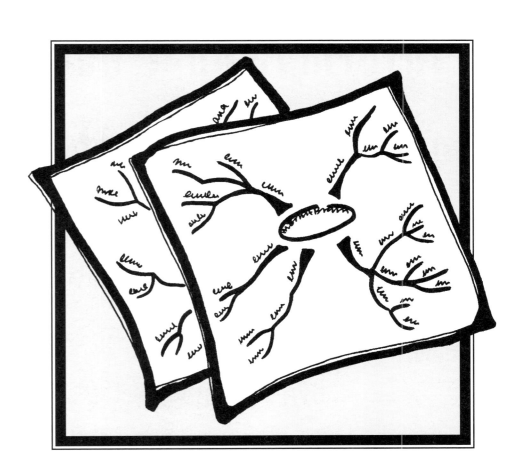

'The mind mapping is such a relief – it gives me a way of sorting out the masses of information I have, it makes revising it all seem possible!'

UFA student

Mind mapping

Mind maps are an excellent tool for effective learning. Mind maps stimulate both right and left hemispheres of the brain and the combination of language, logic, colour and images makes this an excellent memory tool. Used correctly they reflect the way the brain naturally organises information.

They can be used to:

- Record a lot of information in a small amount of space
- Generate new ideas and organise them at the same time

This makes mind mapping a great revision tool.

It is important to try to stick to the rules of mind mapping in order to exploit the full potential of mind maps as a whole-brain tool for revision. Mind maps share some common features with 'spider diagrams', with which many teachers are familiar, but they are significantly different. In contrast to 'spider diagrams', mind maps use visual techniques to give words or images emphasis in order to build a visually stimulating whole, making them easier to remember. As well as the obvious use of colour, images and space, mind maps incorporate movement by using curved lines, which are visually more stimulating than straight lines. But perhaps the most obvious difference is that mind maps have words printed along the branches rather than at the end. This enables the mind map to grow and flow from the main idea on the thicker branches at the centre to associated ideas radiating out towards thinner branches at the edges.

Mind mapping requires a new way of thinking and exploring and may, therefore, be a slightly uncomfortable experience for some people – it's sometimes difficult to break old habits. However, it is well worth the effort as, once mastered, most people love mind mapping and find it incredibly useful.

'Laws' of mind mapping

- Only plain paper should be used (lines on the paper would distract the eye and not allow you to read the mind map quickly).

- The paper must be used 'landscape' – our horizontal peripheral vision is greater. Using the paper landscape also means writing is more likely to be the right way up.

- Begin with a central image, preferably using three colours. While you are drawing this, the brain is pre-processing relevant information for the rest of the map.

- Thick branches radiate from the centre. Use a different colour for each. Each thick branch can represent a main part of the topic.

- Branches become thinner as they reach the edges as finer details are added.

- Single words (or very short phrases) should be printed clearly along the length of the line (not at the end).

- Symbols, illustrations etc. can be used to create memory associations (remember, 'a picture speaks a thousand words').

- The radiant nature of mind maps means you can add to any of the branches at any time. If you come to a standstill on one line of thought carry on with another – your brain will carry on processing the first unconsciously.

'Common sense is not so common'

Voltaire
French philosopher & writer

The bigger picture

Of course, mind mapping isn't the only way to take and make notes. It is, however, one tool to consider and although we have found young people and adults alike to be very enthusiastic about learning how to mind map there will probably be people who would much rather stick to their own habitual way of doing things. Mind mapping offers one approach underpinned by sound theory, so at the very least we should understand the reasons why many people find it useful and apply some of that reasoning to whatever approaches we choose to adopt. Making linear notes and lists are still valid ways of working.

Suggested reading:

The Mind Map Book   **Tony Buzan**

(Lovely illustrations that are great for showing students the potential of mind maps.)

Map It!   **Nancy Marguiles**

(Kids love the cartoon approach of this comic.)

'Vertical thinking is digging the same hole deeper. Lateral thinking is trying again elsewhere.'

Edward de Bono
authority on creative thinking

Workshop plan

Learning outcomes:

By the end of this workshop students will:
- understand the process of mind mapping
- be able to apply it to their own revision.

Activity 1: What is mind mapping? (15 minutes)

Students explore a mind map of the brain and, through it, begin to work out the laws of mind mapping.

Activity 2: Creating a mind map together (10–15 minutes)

By being taken through the process, students learn to use mind mapping for themselves.

Activity 3: Have a go! (30+ minutes)

Students mind map something they're currently revising.

Review: Two questions (10 minutes)

1. What have we learned in this workshop?
2. How might this help us in our revision in the future?

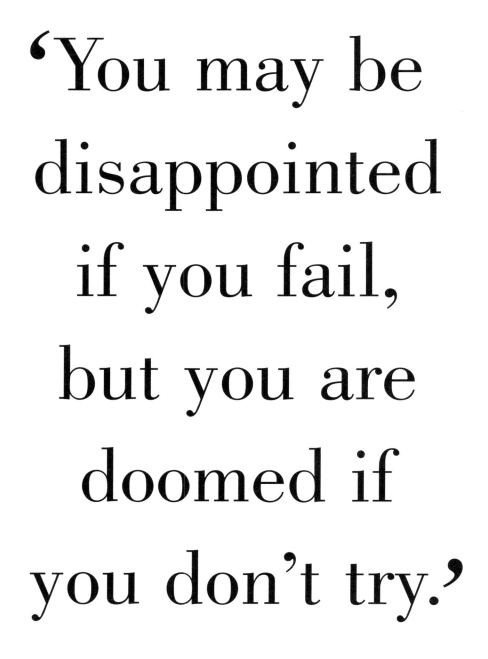

'You may be disappointed if you fail, but you are doomed if you don't try.'

Beverly Sills
American opera singer

Activity 1: What is mind mapping?

Aim/s: For students to explore a mind map and begin to understand how mind maps are constructed and why they are brain friendly.

Resources: *My brilliant brain mind map. Benefits of mind mapping. 'Laws' of mind mapping.*

The activity

1. Ask the students, individually, to look at the mind map 'My brilliant brain' for two minutes and try to get as much information as they can out of it.

2. Now ask them to work with a partner and share that information – talk out what they know from the mind map.

3. After a few minutes ask groups to feed back the information they have extracted.

4. Now ask the students to have a look at how the mind map is constructed. Ask what they think the 'laws' of mind mapping might be. Again, ask them to share with a friend and then feedback to the whole group.

5. Students can then be given the handouts:

   'The benefits of mind mapping'

   'The laws of mind mapping'

   Invite students to skim these to see how many of the benefits and laws they in fact came up with in their own discussions.

6. Re-cap the benefits of mind mapping with the students.

Points to make:

✔ It is very easy to glean a lot of information in a short amount of time from a mind map.

✔ Mind maps are brain friendly – they mirror how our brains work.

✔ Mind maps are great for revision because the use of keywords, colour and images helps us to remember more effectively.

✔ They are very personal – you don't need to be an artist to draw images/symbols that will mean something to you.

✔ You can use colour as an organisational tool – e.g. use one colour for the whole of one main branch and the branches that stem from it. Or, use colours to link with the content e.g. blue can signify cold, the sea etc. whilst red can signify danger, love, heat etc.

❛ I realise I was pushing to get through the content; now I am more aware of uncovering the learning, and mind mapping has helped that. ❜

UFA tutor

'Millions saw the apple fall, but Newton was the one who asked why.'

Bernard M. Baruch
American economist

Activity 2: Creating a mind map together

> **Aim/s:** To take the students through the process of creating a mind map. By modelling the process students can see how the guidelines explored in Activity 1 actually come to life.
>
> **Resources:** White board/OHP. Coloured pens.

The activity

This works really well if you can create a mind map on the board or OHP that all the students will be able to add to. Usually a mind map of a soap opera or a film they have all seen works well. It doesn't matter if you haven't seen it - you will be asking the questions!

It might be worth having a couple of students in charge of making sure you 'stick to the laws' so that if at any time you deviate from the laws of mind mapping they can remind you – you are learning mind mapping with them after all.

Begin the discussion something like this:

What shall we mind map? Think of a soap opera or a film…

…OK, think of a central image for this soap opera…

…Let's add colour to the central image. What colours should we use?

…What is that central image telling us? Is there anything else we ought to add to it?

…OK, what are going to be our main branches?

Students might suggest

- Settings/venues
- Current plot line
- Past plot line
- Families (this is an important one if you're doing a soap opera)
- Other characters
- Audience – who watches it?

You would then go round each main branch and add information in a coherent and linked manner – by asking lots of questions. You don't have to complete the mind map, but do enough to exemplify the process.

Points to make:

- ✔ The beauty of mind maps is that whenever thoughts dry up on one main branch, you just move to another and start thinking about that.
- ✔ Remember to show links between branches as well as within branches, e.g. there may be a link between a character and a setting.

> ❛I liked the mind mapping because I love doodling and it will help me with work in school at the same time.❜
>
> UFA student

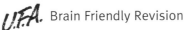

'Shoot for the moon. Even if you miss it you will land among the stars.'

Les Brown
international author

Activity 3: Have a go!

Aim/s: For students to actually experience the process of mind mapping for themselves.

Resources: Paper. Coloured pens. Students' own revision material (see note below).

The activity

Ask the students to try developing their own revision mind map following the guidelines on 'Laws of mind mapping'. Remember to reinforce the 'rules' at every stage.

Note

It is best if students have brought their own revision for this activity but if you feel they need practice with the process before using it for revision purposes ask them to either complete the mind map begun in the last activity or to do a mind map on any of the following:

● a hobby
● my future
● an interest, e.g. sport, music, etc.

If you feel students are lacking in confidence, or if literacy levels are a concern, this activity can be done in pairs.

> 'I am now going to use mind maps to help me with my work.'
> UFA student

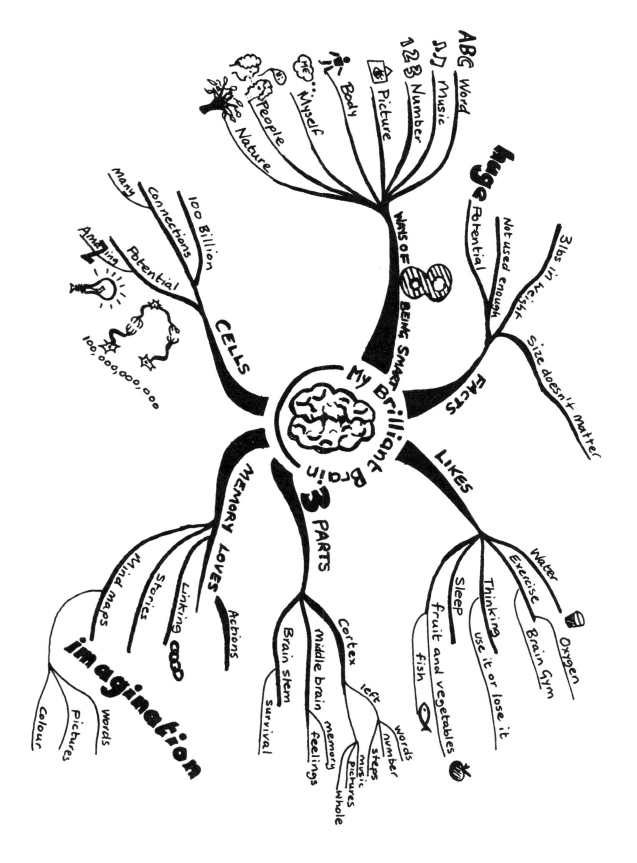

'My brilliant brain'

Benefits of mind mapping

1. Mirrors how the brain looks and works

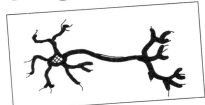

2. Makes use of linking

3. Makes use of different learning styles

4. Ideas are easy to remember

5. Saves time – you only record keywords

6. Stimulates the right (pictures) and left (words) side of the brain

7. Easy to review, easy to recreate from memory – useful for revision

8. Makes use of many different types of intelligence

'Laws' of mind mapping

Everyone creates their own personal style of mind mapping! Use these 'laws' as a guide to help you find your own personal style.

1 Paper
Blank paper.
Landscape not portrait.
Use only one side.

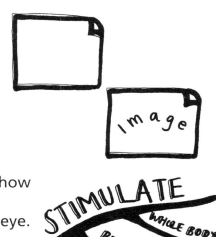

2 Central image
Central image attracts the eye.

3 Branches
Main branches thicker to show importance.
Curved lines – interest the eye.
Length of line = length of word.

4 Words
Only keywords
Main branch word – upper case
Lower branch word – lower case.
Vary size relative to importance.

5 Images
Stimulates the right hemisphere.
Easy to remember.
Attracts the eye.
Eye takes in images faster than words (and remembers them for longer).

6 Colour
Stimulates the right hemishpere.
Use one colour per main branch.

7 Spacing
Leave lots of space so you can add to the mind map.

8 Symbols
Use arrows to guide the eye.
Use symbols (create your own).

9 Personal style
This is important. It is your mind map for YOU.
Develop your own personal mind map style.

10 Have
When learning is fun you learn faster.
When learning is fun you remember it.
Make your mind maps fun.
Have fun doing them!

MY AMAZING MEMORY

'I learned ways of making revision smarter. It was interesting to know what sort of things make revision easier.'

UFA student

My amazing memory

Revision can be a much more positive experience if students are taught to maximise their ability to remember. Your memory is the ability to understand, store and recall information and all learning depends upon it. When students say, 'I don't know how to revise' they often mean that they're not sure how to work so they can remember things. Simple memory techniques are relatively easy to learn and can help to give students an immediate feeling of success and achievement, which can impact on their future exam success.

Your brain will disregard what it doesn't need. Around 70 percent of what you learn in a day is gone in 24 hours – unless you intend to remember it and practise it. To improve your memory you need to create associations between things and stronger pathways from your senses to what you need to remember.

There are three sorts of memory:

1. **Immediate memory** – this holds information for a few seconds or passes it on to your:

2. **Short term or working memory** – this can hold about seven items at one time. If information is not rehearsed immediately, or seen in your head, it will be forgotten in 30 seconds. It sifts, rejects or selects information to go into the:

3. **Long term memory** – This is the storage system; it holds millions of pieces of data. You have several long term memories – including a visual memory, for what you see, an auditory memory for what you hear and a motor memory for what you do.

As you know, our five senses are our learning channels – we can all remember past events by recalling the smell, touch, taste, sound and vision of something. We store memory coming from all our senses. Some people prefer to learn through their visual channel because they have strong connections to their visual memory. Others prefer to learn through their auditory or hearing channel because they have a good connection to their auditory memory and others learn best by doing because they have a good motor memory.

However, by learning in a multi-sensory way, taking information in through all our senses, we can all make learning and remembering easier.

Suggested reading:

Use Your Memory   Tony Buzan
*Change Your Way of Thinking**   Herbie Brennan
*Have a Mega Memory**   Jonathan Hancock

* Great for students

MAKE YOUR LEARNING STICK

Learn a topic

◆ **Repeat within 24 hours**

◆ **Repeat again for 10 minutes at the end of the week**

◆ **Repeat again for 10 minutes two weeks later**

◆ **Repeat again for 10 minutes one month later**

Be successful!

Workshop plan

Learning outcomes:

By the end of the workshop students will have:
- a raised awareness of why we forget things so easily and what this tells us about how our brains work
- explored how their memory works
- explored the use of narrative and visualisation as simple memory tools.

Activity 1: Why do we forget? (30 minutes)

This is a sorting/prioritisation activity in which the students match up statements about why they forget with the explanations for why this might be so. This is a good activity to introduce what we know about the brain and memory in learning. This activity does require a fair bit of reading; groupings need to take this into account.

Activity 2: Check your memory (20 minutes)

This is a memorisation activity which explores some simple ways that we remember things. In the group discussion it is vital to make the implications for revision very explicit.

Activity 3: Linking to remember (10 minutes)

This activity explores the importance of association. Students are shown a collection of objects on a tray and then the tray is covered and the students tested for how many they can recall. After reflecting on how the objects can be linked, the test is done again.

Activity 4: Remembering words through stories (10–20 minutes)

This introduces students to visualisation as a powerful memory tool. Coupled with narrative this becomes a whole-brain learning tool, which can really transform revision. It is important to stress to students that visualisation and the use of narrative get more effective the more you use them.

Activity 5: What do I know? (20+ minutes)

It is important to give students time to reflect on what they have learned and begin to see the uses for revision more clearly. The end product is not nearly as important as the discussion that will be generated.

Review: Sharpening up my memory (20–30 minutes)

This is good for focusing students on many of the learning points from the session. Even if you don't have time for this, it is really useful to use the traffic lights sheets to consolidate what the students are taking away from the session.

DON'T FORGET...

70 percent of what you learn is forgotten in 24 hours;

about 40 percent is forgotten immediately!

YOU MUST REVIEW!

Activity 1: Why do we forget?

> **Aim/s:** An introductory activity that gets students to explore what they know about why they forget things.
>
> **Resources:** *Why I forget – reasons & explanations*. This activity will need to be prepared in advance. The reasons and explanations should be photocopied onto two different colours, cut up and placed in envelopes with the instructions for use pasted onto the front. Laminating will allow you to use this activity over and over again.

The activity

Begin by asking if anyone has ever forgotten something important – how did this make him or her feel? Who would like to know why we forget things?

Pupils can work in pairs or threes. Give each group an envelope which contains the sorting activity. Explain that there are 13 reasons why we might forget things and also explanations as to why pieces of information might not be remembered. Ask the students to:

1. Match the reasons with the explanations.
2. Pick out the top five reasons why they think they personally forget things. Record these on the sheet 'Reasons why I forget'.
3. Using your understanding about why you forget, how might you work to improve your revision? Spend five minutes thinking on your own about your top five reasons why you forget and the explanations that go with them. What action could you take to minimise these?

Points to make:

✔ Our brains are as individual as our fingerprints and our memories are too – your reasons for forgetting things may be different from other people's.

✔ Understanding why we forget takes us one step closer to figuring out how we can make better use of our memory.

✔ Your 'Reasons why I forget' sheet can now form part of a plan for improving your revision.

> ❛It helped them find different ways to approach problems. ❜
>
> Parent of UFA student

The full list of reasons and explanations appears on the following pages.

'Emblazon these words on your mind...

...learning is more effective when it's fun!'

Peter Kline
American educator & author

Why I forget – reasons & explanantions

R **I don't understand.**

E Your long-term memory will not be able to store information it does not understand.

R **I don't take in the information in the first place.**

E If you have poor attention, your brain will not be able to take in the information. If you tell your brain you are not interested in this information, it will not work to help you remember it.

R **I am distracted.**

E When your mind is on other things, the whole of your brainpower can't be put to good use. It is better to try to remember things in short bursts when you are fully concentrating.

R **I don't feel good.**

E If you are tired, anxious or bored you will not be able to remember things well.

R **My mind is muddled.**

E New information can become confused with existing information if you learn similar things at the same time without fully understanding either of them. They will get muddled in your head – e.g. different but related science experiments.

R **I don't want to remember.**

E Unpleasant experiences (e.g. failure in a subject) make learning harder. It is important to try to deal with failure as a chance to learn.

R **I don't have a good way of remembering.**

E This is when you haven't used any memory techniques, pictures or actions to store and then unlock information in your head.

R **I don't rehearse and practise things I need to remember.**

E This is when you have left information before it is fully learned and stored in your brain. You haven't gone over the information enough before storing it in your long-term memory.

R **I don't think it's important enough.**

E You remember those things you attach importance to – you won't remember what you had for your tea this day last year, but you will probably remember what happened on your birthday.

R **I don't organise things in my own head to make it easier to remember.**

E This is when you try to cram in too much information into your memory without sorting it and making sense of it first. It all becomes a big jumble.

R **I don't come back to my learning often enough to keep it in my head.**

E This happens when you don't go over the information for a long time and therefore don't give your brain chance to revisit the information in your long-term memory. After a while it will get lost unless you practise going over it.

R **I don't look after my brain enough.**

E Your brain needs lots of water to help it to pass messages backwards and forwards quickly.

R **I feel anxious when I have to remember in exams.**

E If you are feeling anxious your 'thinking brain' may begin to shut down and it will be so much harder to retrieve anything from your memory.

'The more you link, the more you learn'

Jeanette Vos
international educator & author

Activity 2: Check your memory

> **Aim/s:** To test memory skills and illustrate the
> effectiveness of various simple memory techniques.
> **Resources:** Baroque music (see p.242)

Initial activity

Explain that this session will try out the group's memory skills – how good are they at remembering and how do they remember?

1. Ask the group to sit quietly and listen to the following words. They must not interrupt. You are going to ask them to remember as many as possible. You will read the list only once.

1. Car	17. Garden
2. Honesty	18. Cart
3. Chips	19. Washing
4. Black	20. Hate
5. Computer	21. Calculator
6. School	22. Yellow
7. The	23. Box
8. Green	24. Desk
9. CD	25. Love
10. Bicycle	26. The
11. Robbie Williams	27. Tape
12. Revenge	28. Floor
13. Fish	29. Plane
14. Teacher	30. Red
15. Salt	31. The
16. The	32. Playground

2. Working individually, allow the students three minutes to see how many of those words they can remember. Make it clear that this is not a test. It doesn't matter how many they can remember, just see how they get on. Perhaps play some slow Baroque music (see p.242) while the students remember the words.

3. Ask the students how many of the words they have remembered. Which words can they remember? As each student suggests a word ask them why they remembered that word. Ask the other students how many of them remembered the same word.

'One of the most profound miracles of the human brain is our capacity for memory.'

Jean Houston
American philosopher & educator

Points to make:

In general the following memory points should come out in discussion:

✔ You remember the words at the beginning and at the end – it's the ones in the middle that get lost – why?

✔ It helps to make categories of words in your mind – colours, modes of transport, moods.

✔ It helps to make links or associations – fish, chips, peas, salt and vinegar

✔ It helps if words are repeated – 'the'.

✔ Some words stand out – dinosaur.

✔ Some words have a strong image, and maybe sounds associated with them, e.g. 'Robbie Williams'.

✔ Some words have strong emotions attached to them, e.g. 'exams'.

4. Now try this memory activity again, using the new list of words. This time ask the students to try to focus on listening for categories and see how many they can remember now. Explain that there are four categories of words in this list. (You may or may not decide to tell them what the categories are – it is easier if the brain is primed to listen for categories rather than having to make the categories up as they listen. The categories are: food, buildings, transport, numbers. There are ten in each category, but don't let them know that at this stage.)

The new list of words to remember

1.	Rice	21.	Restaurant
2.	Church	22.	Twenty-five
3.	Fifty	23.	School
4.	Plane	24.	Castle
5.	Five	25.	Cheese
6	Chips	26.	Rollerblades
7.	Hot air balloon	27.	Bus
8.	Pizza	28.	Shop
9.	Fifteen	29.	Butter
10.	Curry	30.	House
11.	Bicycle	31.	Twenty
12.	University	32.	Scooter
13.	Burgers	33.	Eggs
14.	Yacht	34.	Lighthouse
15.	Biscuits	35.	Car
16.	Ten	36.	Hospital
17.	Cinema	37.	Forty-five
18.	Train	38.	Thirty
19.	Yoghurt	39.	Thirty-five
20.	Hovercraft	40.	Forty

❛It's about realising that you can use lots of techniques, trying to tap into kids and help them see that they can do it.❜

UFA tutor

Memory

One, I listen or look with care.

Two, I repeat to myself what's there.

Three, I try another way: touch or do or see or say.

Four, with something else I link. This reminds me when I can't think.

Five, I group or put into line,

and so I make the idea MINE.

5. Now spend time seeing how many students remembered more than last time.

Points to make:

✔ Most people will have remembered more the second time round because they will have categorised the items on the list and will have tried out some of the suggestions above for remembering them.

✔ In effect, you reduced the number of things you were asking your brain to remember from 40 to four. If your brain remembered the four categories it will then have used this technique as a way of organising the words meaningfully. Mind maps can work in a similar way – if you remember the main branches then much of the information on the subsidiary branches will be remembered by association.

How might you use this knowledge about how your memory works when you are revising?

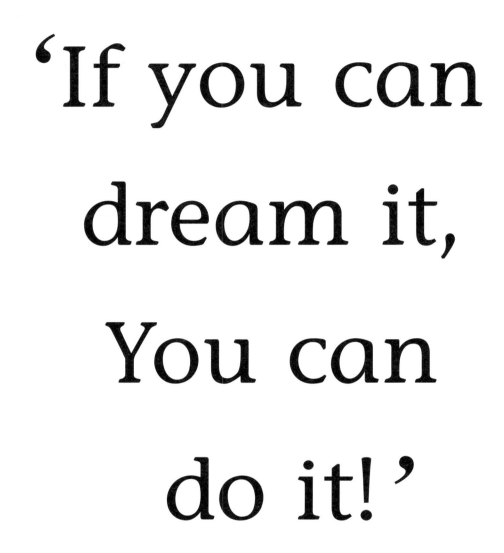

'If you can dream it, You can do it!'

Walt Disney

Activity 3: Linking to remember

Aim/s: To show the importance of association for memory, as well as showing that different people will remember things in different ways by making different associations.

Resources: 10–20 assorted everyday objects (a range, so as not to fall into obvious categories). A cloth large enough to cover the objects.

10 mins

The activity

1. Show students a range of 10 to 20 objects you have collected together. Try to include some quite small and some larger objects. Allow the students to look at the objects for a couple of minutes to see how many they will be able to remember.

2. Cover the objects.

3. Ask students to write down individually as many as they can remember. If literacy is a concern, students can work in pairs with one talking out loud and the other counting how many have been remembered.

4. As a whole group, look at the objects again. Discuss ways of pairing up or grouping the objects using whatever criteria they wish. For example, a cup could be paired with a bottle of water because you drink the water using the cup. A cup could be paired with a glass because you can drink from both. The possibilities are endless and there are no wrong answers; as long as there is an association in the student's head it will work. To make this a more active discussion, students can be asked to move the objects next to each other and explain how they would link them. Work out pairings or groupings for all the objects.

5. Cover them up again.

6. Ask students to see how many they can remember this time.

Points to make:

✔ Memory LOVES linking.
✔ If you remember one object, your memory automatically links it to the other object you linked it to.
✔ It is important to introduce, show and reinforce the following words:

MEMORY
LINK
ASSOCIATION

'Claire remembered various tasks which she was eager to share with me.'
Parent of UFA student

Some statistics to consider...

We remember:

20%	of what is said
30%	of what we hear
40%	of what we see
50%	of what we say
60%	of what we do
90%	of what we see, hear, say and do.

Activity 4: Remembering words through stories

Aim/s: To introduce stories as another powerful memory tool.
Resources: None.

The activity

Another way to remember words, particularly if you need to remember them in order is to link them into a story and to visualise the story. Try this one as a way to remember a shopping list. Next time you have to fetch something from the shops try to go without a list and exercise your memory!

1. Ask students to sit quietly while you read out the following shopping list:

Milk	Cheese
Tomatoes	Matches
Paper towels	Cornflakes
Jam	Sausages
Soap	Bin liners

2. Ask them to close their eyes and listen to this story, and as they do so ask them to try to visualise themselves doing these things:

    *One day I was thirsty and so I reached in the fridge for a carton of **milk**.*
    *I tried to pour the milk out of the carton but it wouldn't come out. I looked, and the spout of the carton was blocked by an old squishy **tomato**.*
    *I put my finger into the spout and pulled out the tomato. I then had to find something to wipe my hand with and so I reached for a **paper towel**. As usual we had the towel with the little bears on. Suddenly one of the bears came alive, leapt off the towel and started to eat the **jam** straight from the jar. In no time at all it was sticky with sugary jam and I tried to clean its fur. I reached for the **soap** and rubbed and rubbed it but it seemed to get worse – in fact it got really smelly! I looked down and saw that instead of picking up the soap I had picked up a piece of **cheese**. This had made such a smell of cheese that a little mouse popped out of its mouse hole in the corner of the kitchen to have a look.*
    *It was such a sweet little mouse that I started to make it a little house. I made the walls out of **matches** and then squashed **cornflakes** on the roof to make it look like a straw roof. To give it a final touch I stuck a **sausage** on for a chimney. Unfortunately the sausage was too heavy and the whole lot collapsed. I swept the whole sorry mess into a black **bin liner** and went out to the shops. Now what did I need to buy?........*

3. Now invite students to rehearse the story in their heads, trying to remember the words.

4. Check: who can remember the words in order? Remember – lots of claps and cheers when they get it right!

> ❛ When I got to Year 10 the opportunity to get involved as a peer tutor came up – I helped at the Easter revision school for Year 6 SAT students. ❜
>
> UFA student

'To learn anything fast and effectively you have to see it, hear it, feel it.'

Tony Stockwell
Professor of History, Royal Holloway, University of London

U.F.A. Brain Friendly Revision

> ## Points to make:
>
> ✔ Explain why this works. Your memory works like a string of beads – if it remembers one event, this triggers the next event and so on. If the events and the words are linked through a story this is using more of your brain to remember! The zanier the better.

Follow-on

As a practice, imagine you have to remember the following list of words. The five words might be subject headings of a topic you want to revise or passwords for stages in a computer game or keywords to remind you of parts of an essay. The five words you have to remember are:

Walnut, History, Rested, Ruler and Lion.

Step One: Build up a picture for each word, with as many memory-jogging clues as possible. You might want to split a word into smaller words or use similar-sounding ones. Don't forget to use all your senses to build up the picture – what does it look like, sound like, feel like? For example, walnut can be split into wall and nut. The picture you create in your mind might be a wall at school covered in nuts.

Step Two: Put your story-telling skills to the test by connecting all the pictures together. Have fun – make it funny or exaggerated if you want. Using yourself in the story is a great way of attaching emotion and it is easier to remember things about yourself.

Your story might begin like this:

*When I walked into the English classroom, I was shocked to see the **wall** was covered in **walnuts**! Was I going **nuts**? I asked myself. Just as I was about to look closer...*

Ask students to carry on this activity on their own, building up their own story to remember these words. Then ask them to share their story with a partner – it will be interesting to see how the stories are different – or if there were any similarities.

> ## Points to make:
>
> ✔ Your brain will remember images readily. Visualising makes use of the brain's love of images. Linking this to a story also makes use of its capacity for narrative (see Workshop Seven).

Light tomorrow with today!

Activity 5: What do I know?

> **Aim/s:** A useful activity to recap what the students have learnt about memory so far.
>
> **Resources:** You may need to provide resources depending on how you ask the students to feedback their ideas (materials for preparing posters, presentations etc. – see below).

The activity

What advice would you give to a student beginning their revision about the use of their memory?

This activity can be done in groups of three or four with feedback to the whole group at the end or it can be a whole-group discussion session. Group feedback might take the form of a poster, a mini presentation, a role-play etc. depending on how much time you have.

Ask the students to reflect on the activities they have taken part in so far and to think about the following questions, making a note of the ideas the group comes up with:

- What does your memory like doing?
- How long should revision sessions be? (Remember that you are more likely to remember beginnings and ends!)
- How can you make the learning more memorable? (Attach emotion, make it unusual, funny, real etc.)
- How can information be organised? (Split it into chunks that are linked in some way)

Ask the groups to feed back their ideas.

Points to make:

- ✔ Will what we know about how our memories work help us to revise more effectively?
- ✔ This activity in itself will help us to remember more about memory because we are recapping on what we have learnt about memory in lots of different ways.
- ✔ Your revision will be much more effective if you recap. Do this soon after you have learnt something and go back to it regularly. Regular recapping takes less time than if you leave everything to the last minute, as you will be able to remember things more readily.

> ❛ Everything I have learnt I have tried out and I can continually change and learn. ❜
>
> UFA tutor

'A mind stretched by a new idea never returns to its original dimensions.'

Oliver Wendell Holmes
former American judge

Review: Sharpening up my memory

> **Aim/s:** To focus students on the learning points from the session and help them to set some personal goals.
>
> **Resources:** *Sharpening up my memory/Traffic lights* (one per student).

The activity

Using the student sheet 'Sharpening up my memory' ask the students to:

- Underline in green up to three things they will certainly try out.

- Underline in amber up to three things they will continue to do/might have a go at.

- Underline in red up to three things they don't think they will use, that are just not for them.

These can be recorded on the traffic lights section (start, continue, stop).

This is best done as an individual exercise and will help students take forward personal goals from this workshop.

⁶ This is your choice and nobody can make it for you! ⁹

UFA student

The essence of knowledge is, having it, to apply it; not having it, to confess your ignorance.

Confucius
Chinese philosopher

Why do we forget ?

The following are the instructions for the activity and should be stuck onto the front of the envelopes containing the statements.

In this envelope there are:

13 reasons why you might forget things.

13 explanations about why pieces of information are not remembered.

First match the reasons with the explanations.

Then, pick out the top five reasons why you think you personally forget things.

In this envelope there are:

13 reasons why you might forget things.

13 explanations about why pieces of information are not remembered.

First match the reasons with the explanations.

Then, pick out the top five reasons why you think you personally forget things.

Why I forget – reasons

I don't understand	I don't take in the information in the first place
I am distracted	I don't feel good
My mind is muddled	I don't want to remember

U.F.A. Brain Friendly Revision

I don't have a good way of remembering

I don't rehearse and practise things I need to remember

I don't think it's important enough

I don't organise things in my own head to make it easier to remember

I don't come back to my learning often enough to keep it in my head

I don't look after my brain enough

I feel anxious when I have to remember in exams

Why I forget – explanations

Your long term memory will not be able to store information it does not understand.

If you have poor attention, your brain will not be able to take in the information. If you tell your brain you are not interested in this information, it will not work to help you remember it.

When your mind is on other things, the whole of your brain power can't be put to good use. It is better to try to try remember things in short bursts where you are fully concentrating.

If you are feeling anxious, you will close down the thinking brain and it will be so much harder to get anything from your memory.

New information can become confused with existing information if you learn similar things at the same time without fully understanding either of them. They will get muddled in your head – e.g. different but related science experiments.

Unpleasant experiences (e.g. failure in a subject) will make learning harder. It is important to try to deal with failure as a chance to learn.

This is when you haven't used any memory techniques, pictures or actions to store and then unlock information in your head.

This is when you have left information before it is fully learned and stored in your brain. You haven't gone over the information enough before storing it in your long term memory.

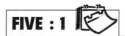
You remember those things you attach importance to – you won't remember what you had for your tea this day last year, but you will probably remember what happened on your birthday.

This is when you try to cram in too much information into your memory without sorting it and making sense of it first. It all becomes a big jumble.

This happens when you don't go over the information for a long time and therefore don't give your brain chance to revisit the information in your long term memory. After a while it will get lost unless you practise going over it.

Your brain needs lots of water to help it to pass messages backwards and forwards quickly.

If you are feeling anxious your 'thinking brain' may begin to shut down and it will be so much harder to retrieve anything from your memory.

Sharpening up my memory

When you are asked to learn something try these ideas:

Listen to instructions carefully before you start learning something so that you know exactly what is important in this new learning and what you should paying full attention to.

Create interest – find a reason why you should be interested in learning this. What's in it for you?

Understand it – make sure you understand the information. Ask a friend to explain it to you or try to explain it to someone else – this is the best way to find out if you really understand it. If you don't understand, go back to your teacher or to a friend and keep asking questions until you do understand it.

Concentrate – set yourself time limits for learning and concentrating. 10–15 minutes at a time is good, then stand and have a stretch, walk around and come back to it a few minutes later. Use Brain Gym® to help you to wake up your brain!

Rehearse it out loud – speak out what you are learning, put it to music, make a tape and play it back.

Make a picture to remind you – use colours and pictures to help you to remember things.

Organise information into chunks – learn 'chunks' at a time – don't try to learn lots of unconnected information, as your brain will find it impossible to remember it.

Create associations – link new learning with learning that has gone before – this helps the brain to make links with what it already knows.

Build in unusual information – the brain will remember anything that is different, spooky, strange or funny – so build this in wherever you can.

Use your body – write things out on post-its or cards, and shuffle them, re-order them, stick them up on the wall, walk around while you are rehearsing the information in your head. Movement and learning are linked.

Be relaxed – try playing some relaxing music. Experiment with Baroque music – research shows that it has an effect on brain waves – strange but true!

Make your visual images of facts varied and interesting – use colourful flash cards, memory maps, charts, diagrams, and posters – anything to stimulate the brain.

Return to the learning regularly – stick posters and memory maps around the place, have keywords on flash cards so you can return to the information regularly and your brain can have lots of chances to 'hook into' the information and refresh the memory bank.

Now check with a friend:

What were their 'greens'?   – Go for it!
What were their 'ambers'?   – Maybe…?
What were their 'reds'?   – Stop, no good for me!

Traffic lights

To help with my revision…

I'm going to stop…

I'm going to continue…

I'm going to start…

U.F.A. Brain Friendly Revision

LEARNING STYLES
& HOW TO USE THEM

'Now I know what sort of a learner I am, I can revise using my strengths — I'm going to use post-its and tapes to help me.'

UFA student

Learning styles & how to use them

The outside world is perceived by our brain through all of our five senses, but we also have a preference for how we recreate and make sense of that information. For some individuals it will be a **visual** preference, for others **auditory** and for others **kinaesthetic**. To learn effectively we need to have information presented to us in a way that matches our preference. Students will be more able to revise effectively if they are aware of their preferred learning style, whilst understanding that effective revision engages all the senses.

If you have a **visual** preference then you will find it easy to build up mental pictures. You readily 'see' yourself operating in different contexts. You'll see images associated with words or feelings and they will affirm your understanding of new information only when you see it happen or see it written or described visually. When spelling you may 'see' the word as you are about to write it out.

If you have an **auditory** preference, it is expressed through a preference for internal dialogue and through language generally. You may 'hear' the word spelled out before writing it. In anticipating a new situation, you may have a mental rehearsal of what will be said by and to you.

With a **kinaesthetic** preference you will often use strong emotional attachments. In spelling a word you may feel yourself writing it letter by letter beforehand or it may simply feel right.

Visual	• The use of yourself and your body movements • Utilising the visual display opportunities above eye level within the room • Video, OHP, slides, flip chart, coloured board markers or chalk • Lively and engaging textbooks • Memory mapping, collage and visual note-taking tools • Keywords displayed around the room
Auditory	• Paired and group discussion, group reviews • Guest speakers • Mini-debates • Raps, rhyme, chants and verse, dramatic readings • Tapes, sound-bites • Mnemonics, onomatopoeia • Music for energising, relaxing, visualising and review
Kinaesthetic	• Body sculpture, mime • Gestures or movements learnt to demonstrate a concept • Break-state activities • Design and build activities • Field trips and visits • Physical movement – e.g. Brownian Motion demonstrated by students bumping together in a confined space, maps drawn on hard play areas to help learn countries and trade routes.

Examples of VAK approaches (taken from Alistair Smith, *Accelerated Learning in the Classroom*, NEP, 1996).

Suggested reading:

Accelerated Learning in the Classroom   **Alistair Smith**

LEARNING IN DIFFERENT WAYS

We take in information by:

 Seeing (visual)

 Hearing (auditory)

 Doing (kinaesthetic)

However, the best way to learn is through all your senses at the same time. This is:

Multi-sensory learning.

Workshop plan

Learning outcomes:

By the end of this workshop students will:
● understand that they have Visual, Auditory and Kinaesthetic ways of learning
● be aware of their own preference for making sense of new information
● have explored some Visual, Auditory and Kinaesthetic strategies.

Activity 1: Me and my senses (10–15 minutes)

A brainstorm to help students think about how they take in information from the outside world.

Activity 2: VAK questionnaire (10 minutes)

Students fill in a questionnaire to help to establish their learning style preference.

Activity 3: VAK circus (45–60 minutes)

Students explore visual, auditory and kinaesthetic ways of learning by rotating round three activities and then discuss their findings.

Review: Two questions (10 minutes)

1. What have we learned in this workshop?
2. How might this help us in our revision in the future?

Just do it!

You learn to talk by talking.

You learn to walk by walking.

You learn best by doing it!

Activity 1: Me and my senses

Aim/s: For students to begin to think about how they take in information from the outside world.
Resources: None.

The activity

Ask students to discuss (in pairs) how we take in information from the outside world. Allow five minutes for discussion then ask for pairs to feedback to the whole group. How many of these senses do we use when we're revising?

Points to make:

✔ Multi-sensory learning engages more of our senses and will be more effective in the long run. Our brains are designed to process our experience of the world. We take on amazing amounts of information from the world around us using our senses. Sometimes learning can be sensory-dull – we need to make it sensory-rich and stimulating.

6 It was brilliant. It opened a new chapter in my learning career. 9

UFA student

'Each one teach one'

Marian Diamond
Professor of Anatomy, University of California, Berkeley

Activity 2: VAK questionnaire

Aim/s: This questionnaire aims to assess people's preference for taking on and making sense of new information.

Resources: *VAK questionnaire* for each student.

The activity

Ask students to fill in the VAK questionnaire as honestly as possible and then count up their scores to discover their preferred learning style. As with the Multiple Intelligence questionnaire in the 'My Amazing Intelligence' workshop, this questionnaire may be completed in a number of different ways (see page 55).

Once the questionnaire has been completed, you may like to ask for a show of hands to gauge the range of different preferences across the group – perhaps ask the group for three different ways of feeding back this information. How could they do it visually, auditorily and kinaesthetically?

Points to make:

✔ We all take in information using all three sensory modalities.

✔ Most people have a preference.

✔ The best learning is multi-sensory – using Visual, Auditory and Kinaesthetic approaches.

> ❝ After the session I talked all my history notes onto tape and listened to it when I was in bed or walking to school. It's really helped me. ❞
>
> UFA student

Tell me –
I'll forget.
Show me –
I may remember.
But involve me
and I will
understand.

Chinese proverb

Activity 3: VAK circus

45-60 mins

> **Aim/s:** The idea of this activity is that students work on the same subject matter in three different ways, experiencing all three ways of approaching the same learning. By doing this they are able to compare the ways in which they have interacted with what they are trying to learn and remember.
>
> **Resources:** *Workstation instructions*. Select subject matter closely linked to the students' revision (some straightforward content that students need to revise, e.g. for English Literature it might be characters' names and descriptions, or for Geography a range of vocabulary linked to a particular topic). Multiple copies needed for each workstation (ideally a taped version for the auditory station). Cassette player. Coloured pens. Highlighter pens. Plain paper. Post-it notes.

The activity

Set up three workstations (see below) in the room or in three different rooms. In small groups, students spend 10–15 minutes on each activity and then move on to the next until they have tried all three. The activity ends with the students coming back together for a group discussion around the usefulness of these different approaches.

Visual workstation

1. Draw a mind map of your revision material (see Workshop Four pp.113–128 for instructions).
2. Represent the main facts/concepts as a diagram.
3. Use a highlighter to highlight the key words you need to learn. Trace each word in the air.
4. Try to create a guided visualisation of your revision topic for other members of your group – try it out on them and see how much they can remember.

> *Being involved in activities in different environments enables a child to be aware of his or her capabilities and their contributions to group activities.*
>
> Parent of UFA student

Make your revision colourful!

Auditory workstation

(if possible pre-record any text onto tape for students to listen to as well as read)

1. With a partner read the text aloud paying close attention to the way it sounds. Now try reading it to yourself 'under your breath'.
2. Devise questions to ask about the text and then question a member of your group (take it in turns).
3. Make up a role-play.
4. Decide on the key words/concepts that you will need to learn. Experiment with different ways of saying the key words out loud (emphasise different parts of the word, using different voices).
5. Make up a mnemonic to remember the important facts/concepts.

Kinaesthetic workstation

1. Go for a walk or move around as you read through the text.
2. Write out the main points on index cards and then assemble the cards in a logical order.
3. Using 'post-it' notes write down the main points and devise questions about the text. Assemble the 'post-its' on the wall to see how different areas relate to each other.
4. With your group construct a model or picture to represent the main points.
5. Decide on the key words/concepts that you will need to learn. Write out the words in colour then circle or underline them. Now make up actions to go with the key words you will need to learn – this can be done in pairs or individually and then shared with the group.

Feedback/discussion

● Think about the result of your questionnaire. Did your experience of the VAK activities fit with your preferred learning style?
● How many of these strategies would/could you use in your revision?
● Can you think of any other ways of approaching your revision that would tie in with your preferred learning style?
● Do you think you have a good understanding of this subject having explored it in three different ways?
● If you made your revision V, A and K would it help?

> ‘We used these brain-based revision techniques over three intensive days in the vacation with 19 targeted students (borderline level 3/4) at the end of KS2 in English, Maths and Science. The group achieved 6 level 3 grades, 40 level 4 grades and an astounding 11 level 5 grades. We were thrilled! ’
>
> UFA tutor

'A year from now you may wish you had started today.'

Karen Lamb

VAK questionnaire

Tick the box which describes you best:

1. When you think about spelling a word, do you...

   V. See the word ☐

   A. Sound the word out ☐

   K. Write the word down to see if it looks right ☐

2. When you are really concentrating, are you distracted by...

   V. Messiness/untidiness ☐

   A. Noise/talking/music ☐

   K. Movement ☐

3. When you recall specific incidents, do you...

   V. Do it with pictures/images ☐

   A. Sounds ☐

   K. See moving pictures ☐

4. When you are angry, do you...

   V. Remain silent, but seethe inside ☐

   A. Shout loudly ☐

   K. Clench your fists, grit you teeth, stamp about ☐

5.   When you forget an incident that has happened or a person you've met, do you...

   V.   Forget names but remember faces

   A.   Forget faces but remember names

   K.   Remember only where you were and what you did

6.   When describing an object, for example your front door, would you...

   V.   Picture it in your mind

   A.   Describe it with words

   K.   Think how it feels, sounds, opens etc.

7.   When you are learning, do you prefer...

   V.   Work that is written down in many colours

   A.   Listening to a person talk or give instructions

   K.   Participating in activities, making or doing

8.   When you do leisure activities, do you prefer to...

   V.   Watch TV, read, play on a computer

   A.   Listen to music

   K.   Play sports and games

9.   When you are talking, do you…

V.   Talk little and are reluctant to listen for too long

A.   Like to listen and talk as well

K.   Talk with your hands and gesture a lot

10.   When you receive praise or a reward, do you prefer to…

V.   Receive a written note or certificate

A.   Hear it said to you

K.   Be given a 'pat on the back' or a handshake.

Total no of Vs

Total no of As

Total no of Ks

The letter that has the highest score indicates your preferred way of learning. Many people do not have a really strong preference and can work easily with all three styles – if you have roughly equal scores this may be you!

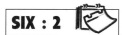

Visual workstation instructions

👁 Draw a mind map

👁 Represent the main facts/concepts as a diagram.

👁 Use a highlighter to highlight the key words you need to learn. Trace each word in the air.

👁 Try to create a guided visualisation for other members of your group – try it out on them.

Auditory workstation instructions

With a partner read the text aloud, paying close attention to the way it sounds. Now try reading it to yourself 'under your breath'.

Devise questions to ask about the text and then question a member of your group (take it in turns).

Make up a role-play.

Decide on the key words/concepts you will need to learn. Experiment with different ways of saying the key words out loud (emphasise different parts of the word, using different voices).

Make up a mnemonic to remember the important facts/concepts.

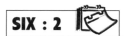
Kinaesthetic workstation instructions

 Go for a walk or move around as you read through the text.

 Write out the main points on index cards and then assemble the cards in a logical order.

 Using 'post-it' notes, write down the main points and devise questions about the text. Assemble the 'post-its' on the wall to see how different areas relate to each other.

 With your group construct a model or still picture to represent the main points.

 Decide on the key words/concepts you will need to learn. Write out the words in colour and circle/underline them. Now make up actions to go with the key words you will need to learn (this can be done in pairs or individually and then shared with the group).

U.FA. Brain Friendly Revision

WORKSHOP SEVEN

VISUALISATION

'I was learning and having fun at the same time.'

UFA student

Visualisation

A picture speaks a thousand words

The underlying principles of an excellent memory are:

- **Imagination**
- **Association**

Using your mind's eye to create pictures can have a profound effect on your ability to recall information. This process of creating images in your head is called **visualisation**. But visualisation involves more than seeing only pictures in your mind. You should also be able to imagine sounds, textures, tastes and smells. The brilliant thing about using your imagination is that anything can happen, which allows you to use exaggeration and humour, both of which make the experience more memorable. Research has shown that using positive and pleasant images for visualisation is more effective because the brain may be more reluctant to return to negative images.

The better you can visualise, the more powerful your memory will become. Visualisation can be used in a variety of ways in learning; to stimulate and anchor the learning when it first takes place and as a tool for recall. For revision purposes we are going to concentrate on the latter. The ability to use your imagination and visualise is something that gets better with practice, although some people do find it easier than others.

Linking what needs to be remembered to something that is stable and constant in the mind is establishing **association**. Therefore, linking new learning to old can speed up recall. Using narrative helps to add the further dimension of sequence and order.

Seeing in our physical world is also a powerful channel for learning. We learn unconsciously as well as consciously. Therefore, posters, post-it notes, mind maps etc. displayed everywhere possible means that students are learning even when they think they are not. Our brains love colour! It's easily memorable and is a great organisational tool for revision. Students should be encouraged to flood their environment with visual material, to use highlighter pens and to try their hand at drawing cartoons, pictures, mind maps etc.

Suggested reading:

Use Your Memory	Tony Buzan
*Change Your Way of Thinking**	Herbie Brennan
*Have a Mega Memory**	Jonathan Hancock

* Great for students

'The only way to predict the future is to invent it.'

Alan Kay
American computer scientist

Workshop plan

Learning outcomes:

By the end of the workshop students will have:
- Explored the potential of their imagination
- Tried out three different memory systems that they can use in their revision

Activity 1: Work the imagination (15–30 minutes)

It is important to establish at the beginning of the session the importance of the imagination in improving your memory. This is a warm-up activity designed to show students how powerful their imagination can be. Students will need to feel secure enough to close their eyes, so they need a little space around themselves. Background Baroque music will be useful to aid concentration. The students are asked to create mental images in their heads. Initially, they do this individually and then move on to work with a partner.

Activity 2: Using the body to remember (15 minutes)

This uses a body locus system for recall and retention. In this activity the students are invited to look at a number of objects which they have to memorise. They are then talked through placing the objects on a person in their imagination. Their recall is tested to see if it has improved using this system.

Activity 3: Using your home to remember (optional, 20 minutes)

This place locus system can either be done in addition to the previous activity or in place of it depending on the needs of the students. It builds upon the previous activity, providing a more substantial locus system, using a house as the constant.

Activity 4: Remembering numbers (30 minutes)

This activity allows students to develop a personal system for remembering numbers, combining story-telling with visualisation. The system will become more effective the more it is used.

Review: Two questions (10 minutes)

- What have we learned in this workshop?
- How might this help us with our revision in the future?

'Imagination is the highest kite that one can fly.'

Lauren Bacall
former Hollywood actress

Activity 1: Work the imagination

Aim/s: For students to explore the power of their imagination and begin to understand how useful it is as a tool to aid memory.

Resources: Baroque music (see p.242). Cassette/CD player.

15-30 mins

The activity

Ask the students to find a space in the room where they can sit comfortably in a small place of their own. Tell them that in a moment you will be asking them to close their eyes. Try playing some Baroque music quietly in the background.

Now ask the students to create a mental picture of the following things with their eyes closed. Encourage them to create as realistic a picture as possible, using all their senses. They should use all the time they are given to build up the image. Some of the images are, initially, harder than others. It is important to give students time to settle into each separate scene. You may want to prompt them by asking them a few questions, e.g. *What can you see? Look in detail at colour, form, texture. How do you feel? How does your body feel? Be aware of all your different senses.*

1. Yourself sitting in the room where you sleep.
2. Your school bag on a table.
3. The taste of a freshly cut lemon.
4. Your hand being plunged into ice-cold water.
5. Being hit with a feather pillow.
6. Putting your hand into some soil in the garden.
7. The taste of lemonade.
8. An empty classroom.
9. The taste of chocolate ice cream.
10. Stepping out of a heated house into the street in the middle of winter.

Notice their reactions as they visualise. For example, many often grimace when recreating the lemon taste (even though there is nothing physically there!). Some people claim that they actually 'tasted' the lemonade – that's the power of the imagination. Our brains don't distinguish between real and imagined scenes – our imagination is that powerful.

Feedback/discussion

Gather the students' reactions to this activity. How easy or difficult did they find it? How powerful do they think their imagination is? How can their imagination be useful in learning/revision?

‘ As a result of today I am going to try to have more confidence in myself and be proud of my abilities and myself at all times. ’

UFA student

Try visualising

Making a mental picture is something everyone can do; visualising is using your mind's eye, mind's ear and mind's feelings to remember.
It's multi-sensory.
It is a mental movie.
It will improve your memory.

Try it!

Extension activity

This can be extended with students working in pairs. Each pair sits facing one another. One prompts the other to create a mental picture, then the other has a go. It is important for the students to work with somebody with whom they feel comfortable.

Points to make:

✔ The imagination is so powerful that it can recreate a sensation/picture in our minds that is almost real.

✔ Our imagination gets better the more we use it.

✔ Our imagination is a very powerful tool that can help us improve our memory and we can use this tool for revision. The next activity begins to show us how we can do this.

'We need to make
the world safe
for creativity and
intuition, for it is
creativity and
intuition that will
make the world
safe for us.'

Edgar Mitchell
Apollo astronaut

Activity 2: Using the body to remember

Aim/s: To introduce the students to one technique for visualisation.

Resources: 10–15 miscellaneous objects such as those listed below (arrange them either on a tray or on a table – it doesn't matter as long as you are able to cover them up/take them away).

The activity

Show the students a range of objects and give them a minute to see how many of them they can remember. It doesn't really matter what the objects are, so for example you may have the following:

A cup and saucer	A pink shoe
An elastic band	A bunch of flowers
A newspaper	A furry teddy bear
A telephone	Three glasses
A cheese roll	A paperclip

Show the collection of objects to the students – how many did they remember?

Now ask the students to imagine a person they know very well (a teacher, parent or themselves will work brilliantly). First ask them to just visualise the person you are going to use. For this exercise we will presume the students are using themselves. Now…

1. Imagine the cup and saucer (**first item** of any list) on the **top of your head**.

2. Imagine the elastic band, which has grown to gigantic proportions (**next item**) pasted onto your **forehead**.

3. The rolled-up newspaper (**Item 3**) is stuffed up your **nose**.

4. The telephone (**Item 4**) goes in your **mouth**.

5. A cheese roll (**Item 5**) can clearly be seen inside your **throat**, which you can visualise as a transparent cylinder.

6. A pink shoe (**Item 6**) is stuck to your **left arm**.

7. A bunch of flowers (**Item 7**) are dropped onto your **chest**.

8. A cute furry teddy (**Item 8**) is tied to your **belly button**.

9. Three glasses (**Item 9**) are balanced on your **right foot**.

10. A huge glittery paperclip (**Item 10**) is placed **under your left foot**.

'He looked forward to going every day and seemed to really enjoy it.'

Parent of UFA student

The only dumb question is the question you don't ask.

Visualise the item you want to remember in or on a particular part of the body. Always do this in the same sequence, starting with the top of the head. There's no need to concentrate or try to remember. As long as you visualise clearly your brain will do the rest.

Remove the items again and once more ask the students to use this technique to recall what was there. Now see how many of the objects they can remember.

Note

We have only used ten items but there are many more parts you can use. Don't forget you can exaggerate the size of objects. The funnier or more unusual the image becomes, the more memorable it is. Just as we have made the throat transparent, other parts of the body can also be given similar treatment.

Feedback/discussion

Does this system make remembering easier? Why? When wouldn't this work?

Follow-on

What if your list contained actions not just objects? For example:

> Fix the vacuum cleaner
> Buy some ice cream
> Post a letter to a friend
> Take the dog to the vet
> Find out what's on at the cinema

Although these actions are very different to each other, they all have one thing in common: they involve at least one object. Once you can extract the object from the action you can use the system as before.

Ask the students to extract the objects from the above, and repeat the activity.

Points to make:

✔ If you remember the things associated with the action, you will automatically remember the action you wanted to take with them.

'Every child is an artist – the problem is how to remain an artist when you are grown up.'

Pablo Picasso
Spanish artist

Activity 3: Using your home to remember

Aim/s: To introduce the students to another technique for visualisation. This builds on the previous activity, providing a more substantial locus system.

Resources: 10–15 miscellaneous objects such as those listed below.

The activity

We have suggested the following list of objects for this activity but it can be adapted to suit your purposes:

Deck of cards	Screwdriver
Gold ring	CD player
Ice cream	Apple tree
Bowl of soup	Playstation magazine
Zebra	Yellow hat
Polar bear	Needle
Paperclip	Poster of pop star

1. Again, you need to ask the students to sit quietly and close their eyes and build up a picture in their minds.

*Imagine yourself standing outside a front door. Try to visualise it as vividly as possible, noting the colour of the paint, the position of the door bell etc. Place **a deck of cards** in front of the door. The only problem is that you might not see such a small object on the floor. So, solve that problem by imagining them as huge, so big that you have to climb over them to get to the front door.*

*Having climbed over the deck of cards and opened the front door you step into the hall. Here you place a **gold ring**. But again the object is small and it might not get noticed amongst all the other things in the hall. To make sure you remember the one you want, put it on the floor, make it sparkle and make it huge as well.*

*There are three doors leading out of the hallway; one right, one left and one straight ahead. Turn right and walk through the door into the living room. **A polar bear** is already sitting in your favourite seat eating an ice cream. You take the **ice cream** away and give him a **bowl of soup**.*

Leading from the living room is a door to the kitchen, where you see the zebra standing on top of the kitchen table. One of the three doors out of the kitchen leads to

> ‘ This seemed to be an ideal opportunity to learn new skills. ’
>
> Parent of UFA student

'*Go confidently in the direction of your dreams! Live the life you've imagined.*'

Henry David Thoreau
American essayist & poet

a walk-in larder where you leave the **paperclip**. *Once again the paper clip is so small that it might easily get lost – turn it into a six-foot-tall paperclip, which you prop against the door so it will fall down with a clang the minute somebody opens it.*

Etc…

2. Now ask the students to imagine that they are walking into their real homes.

…Imagine your home. Make a picture of this in your mind. For the next few minutes, your home is going to be the place you put things you want to remember.

As you move through the rooms, just imagine the various items on your list in different places. Don't spend a lot of time on one object. Just visualise as clearly as you can, put the item in place, then imagine yourself going to the next room.

Try to avoid boredom because once you get bored your concentration goes. Make your mental picture dramatic, make it silly or amusing. Give it movement and sound and make it colourful. Remember that we put the zebra on the kitchen table rather than just on the floor. Even better, we could have it doing a tap dance!

Allow students five minutes to work with the list to complete the visualisation using their home.

Test: *Put the list away, imagine yourself at the front door. Write down as many of the items from the list as you can.*

Reassure students that they will get better the more they use the technique. They can try testing themselves at the end of the day, week and month!

Feedback/discussion

How can this technique help us with revision? What kind of things might we try to visualise?

Points to make:

✔ We can remember new things easily if we can associate them with things with which we are already familiar.

✔ By making visual pictures in our minds we are using our brain's natural capacity to recall images.

✔ The more bizarre, funny and dramatic our visualisations are, the more likely we are to remember.

✔ If we can make use of visualisation in our revision we may be able to remember things more easily.

'Whether you think you can or you think you can't, you're probably right.'

Henry Ford
American automobile engineer

Activity 4: Remembering numbers

Aim/s: To show how story-telling can be linked to a picture system to help remember numbers.
Resources: Whiteboard/blackboard/flip chart.

The activity

Story-telling and visualisation can work hand in hand to help us remember numbers. Everyone can create a system that is individual to themselves. The trick is to make boring, dull numbers memorable by turning them into amazing pictures. People who win memory competitions use this kind of technique.

Ask the students to start by giving each digit from 0 to 9 an object identity and an associated action.

Begin by doing the first few digits on the board with the whole group – it's useful to draw the objects to make the connections. The students can then work on creating their personal system.

For example: **0**   looks like a ball, a football to me, so that's its identity. I could kick, throw or bounce it (actions).

            1   looks like a paintbrush and I could write, paint or colour with it.

            2   reminds me of a swan that could swim, fly or glide.

When you have finished thinking up objects and actions, your system is ready to use.

Using the system:
Treat any number as a list of separate digits. For example, 87 is **8** and **7**. The idea is to turn these into a memorable story using the objects and actions you have just designed.

So, if you had to remember the number **12**, you could turn the **1** into an action – my action for **1** was **paint**. I could turn the next digit, the **2**, into an object, which for me was a **swan**. Now I have:

          Paint a swan

Bring the story to life. What colour is the paint? Does the swan like being painted? It is easy to turn the picture back into the number you wanted to remember because each object and action can mean only one digit. The more digits you have, the longer the story gets.

> ' I found out that learning was fun and interesting. '
>
> UFA student

Your most valuable asset in learning is a positive attitude.

Bobbi DePorter
American educator & author

Give students a few minutes to practise remembering some numbers using their system. Now ask them to work in pairs. Each person gives their partner a number to remember, which they test them on once they have used their system to learn it. Now try to use this system for a longer number – perhaps your phone number or an important date you have to remember for History?

Feedback/discussion

How did you find this technique?
When do you think you might use it?

Points to make:

✔ This technique, like all the others in this workshop, depends on you making the visualisation come alive. The more you can do this the more useful it will be.

✔ The beauty of this technique is that you only ever need nine pictures/symbols; the trick is to use them well by bringing them to life.

✔ Try to refine your personal number system and continue trying it out with numbers that you need to revise.

'You can do what you have to do, and sometimes you can do it even better than you think you can.'

Jimmy Carter
39th US president

PREPARING FOR EXAMS

'I got ways of helping me to recognise what I am and am not doing when it comes to revision.'

UFA student

U.F.A. Brain Friendly Revision

Preparing for exams

Good revision habits are essential to achieve success in exams, but how students cope with the exam itself is also really important. This workshop aims to cover some of the most important aspects of exam preparation, combining valuable tips for the exam with some practical stress-reducers.

We have always known that a positive attitude and high self-esteem are vital for successful learning to occur. Research tells us that the brain responds best in conditions of high challenge with low stress. The enemy of learning is stress. Stress includes fear and anxiety and results from the desire to terminate or escape from a real or imagined negatively reinforcing experience. The optimal conditions for learning include a positive personal learning attitude where challenge is high and anxiety and self-doubt is low.

Suggested reading:

Thirty days to B's and A's	Eric Jensen
Lightening Learning	J & B O'Brien

'I am never afraid of what I know.'

Anna Sewell
British novelist

Workshop plan

This workshop builds on the 'Getting ready to revise' workshop (pp.85–112), but focuses more on dealing with the actual examinations and the time immediately before and after an exam. It also incorporates some brain exercises and relaxation exercises that can be done in the exam itself, which can be interspersed throughout the workshop. Try to introduce students to a different brain exercise in-between each activity.

Learning outcomes:

By the end of the workshop students will:
- have begun to explore the language of exam questions so that they are more able to focus their answer on the requirements of the exam question
- have a range of useful tips that will help them to deal more effectively with the examination paper
- have acquired a few simple strategies to use in the examination room to deal with stress.

Activity 1: Find your partner (10 –15 minutes)

Students move around the room in an adaptation of this traditional party game – using terminology often used in exam questions, matching terms to their definitions.

Activity 2: Valuable exam tips (30 minutes)

Students explore a range of exam tips and are encouraged to think about which tips will be useful for their own exam preparation.

Activity 3: Self-relaxation exercise (20 minutes)

This activity allows the students to try out a relaxation activity that they can use either in the exam itself or during revision; this can act as both a motivator and as a way of reducing tension. Much of this activity is tutor-led and students need to feel quite secure before they can successfully take part in this. You may find it helpful to use some relaxing music in the background.

Review: What? So what? What now? (10 minutes)

A simple review technique to determine how the skills and information explored in the workshop will be useful in preparing for exams.

Take time to think!

Brain exercises

You can introduce these throughout the workshop. Also encourage students to use Brain Gym® (see Workshop One). These exercises can be done in the exam room.

Release the stress

Put your left ankle over your right knee. Hold your left ankle with your right hand and hold your left foot with your left hand – your hands and legs should now be crossed! Sit calmly, breathe deeply and place your tongue on the roof of your mouth for about a minute.

Switch off the panic

Above your eyebrows on your forehead you have two neuro-vascular points. By keeping your fingers pressed on these points and gently massaging, you will relax and you will be better able to concentrate. Massaging behind your ears can help to relieve stress too.

' My daughter has had a wonderful week, making new friends, getting the brain working without much effort; generally having a wonderful time. '

Parent of UFA student

Go for it!

Activity 1: Find your partner

Aim/s: For students to engage with these key words and match them up with their definitions.

Resources: *Understanding the exam question* (one set to be printed on card and cut up into individual terms and definitions). *Terms & definitions* list (one per student).

The activity

1. Print out the terms and definitions on card and share them out amongst the students.
2. Ask students to circulate and try to match the correct term to its definition.
3. Repeat the process so that students become familiar with a range of terms. One way of doing this would be to have all the statements and definitions in a hat that students then draw from.

Points to make:

✔ Understanding these key terms is very important if you are going to do well in exams.

✔ Examiners often report that students have failed to understand what a question was actually asking them to do.

✔ If we have a better understanding of these words we are more likely to focus on the right way of answering the question.

At the end of the exercise a full list of terms and definitions can be given out to each student for reference.

> *You shouldn't be surprised if you get the same results each year if you continue to do things in the same way.*
>
> UFA tutor

'Never measure the height of a mountain until you have reached the top. Then you will see how low it was.'

Dag Hammarskjöld
Swedish statesman

Activity 2: Valuable exam tips

Aim/s: To encourage the students to interact with a range of exam tips and begin to select what might be useful for them. The activity should help students see how some tips will be more valuable to them than others.

Resources: *'Money'. Exam tips.* This activity will need to be prepared in advance. The Exam tips should be photocopied, cut up and put into envelopes; one for each group of four. Each group will need £100 made up as below. Each student needs an additional £50. Each student will also need a *Summary sheet*.

30 mins

The activity

1. Divide the students into groups of four or five.
2. Give each group 100 UFA pounds and an envelope containing 20 exam tips.
3. The group has to decide which tips to spend their money on. The group may buy eight tips in total. The £100 is made up of 3 × £20, 3 × £10 and 2 × £5 so the students will have to decide how much the tips they have chosen are worth.
4. Each group can feed back which tips they spent their money on and why.

At the end of the activity, give each student a £50 note, and the student sheet containing all the tips. Ask them to decide which tip is worth £50 to them and feed this back to the rest of the main group. Students can take away the sheet containing all the tips.

 Note

This activity could be done as a group exercise without using the money – students could be asked to select the three most/least useful tips.

❝ I thought that today was helpful for me – I now know how to revise for my exams. Thank you. ❞

UFA student

'I never practise, I always play.'

Wanda Landowska
internationally recorded keyboardist

Activity 3: Self-relaxation exercise

Aim/s: For students to take part in a relaxation exercise
that they will be able to recreate in an exam if they
feel they need to.
Resources: Plenty of space.

The activity

Students need to sit somewhere where they have a little private space and where they
feel secure enough to close their eyes.

Use the following script to take the students through the relaxation process:

*The purpose of this exercise is to relax you, to give you a feeling of what success can
be like and to motivate you by thinking of success as achievable rather than as a series
of hurdles to be overcome. Relaxation is important because we lose learning which is
not instinctive or over-learned when we are in a stressful situation. Examination
nerves can be overcome by both over-learning the work so that it does not disappear
under stress but also by learning techniques for relieving stress. It is suggested that
you do these exercises at regular intervals as an activity break and also in the
examination room whilst the papers are being distributed. You should be able to
mentally talk yourself through this exercise.*

Follow this routine:

*Sit with your feet together or a little way apart and both on the ground. Put your
hands on your knees. Close your eyes and sit up straight. Imagine that someone is
pouring jelly very slowly over you ,but it is very nice jelly so you don't feel threatened
by this. However, once it has settled for ten seconds, it begins to set very hard but it
still feels very comfortable. The jelly has now covered your feet and has set and if you
use your mind to imagine really well, you will now be unable to move your feet; they
are rooted firmly to the floor (this image may take some time to develop properly since
your mind is not used to working so hard yet). Continue to really picture the jelly
rising slowly but comfortably up your legs. It has reached your knees so that you
cannot move the bottom part of your legs. It continues to rise slowly and sets as it goes
and now you cannot move your legs at all and your hands are also covered and
unmoveable. The jelly continues to rise. There is no need to worry because when it
gets to your neck it will stop so your face will not be covered. Slowly it keeps rising and
now it is up to your chest so your arms are stuck to your sides and slowly it rises even
further until it covers your neck so you cannot move your head, but then it stops.*

*By now you cannot move at all but the jelly has taken all of the strain out of your body.
It is supporting you so you can relax. Think about the best experience you have ever
had in your life. Re-live that experience and remember what you felt like inside while*

> ❛ It has been fantastic.
> I enjoyed every little bit. ❜
> UFA student

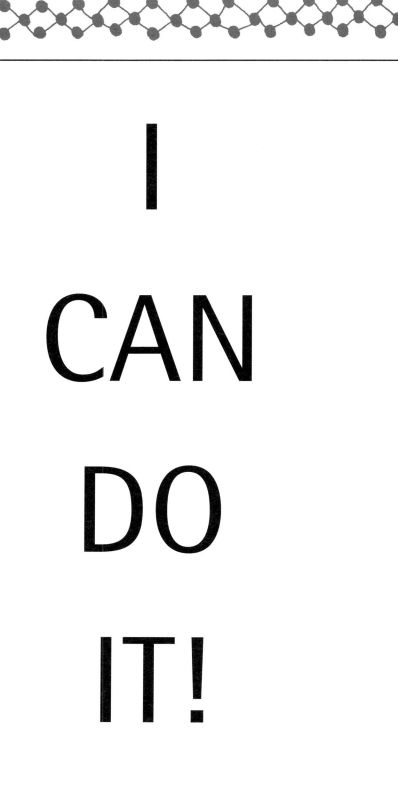

I

CAN

DO

IT!

that was happening. Remember how happy you were and how good you felt. Really re-live the experience until you have that really happy feeling in your mind. Now imagine when the examination results come out and think how great it would be to have that feeling again because you have done better than you ever thought possible. Get the image of that feeling into your brain. Imagine what it would be like to go home and tell your parents or guardians how well you have done. Really enjoy the feeling of success.

Now think of the tasks that you will have to do to get that success. What tasks do you need to do? In what order? Which are the most important tasks? Now think your way through doing those tasks. Think how good you will feel as you do each of the things you know you must do. Think of the success that it will bring and work your way back to results day and the results you will achieve by having done this work.

Now think of a topic you have been learning, for example the characters of a Shakespearean play. Think your way through either just the words or a mind map of what you have been doing. Enjoy the experience of every single thing you remember and do not worry about what you cannot remember (this technique can therefore help you recall information in an examination).

Now gradually bring yourself back into the present. The jelly is gradually dissolving from the top down. You can gently move your head and now your shoulders, now your arms and knees and now your ankles and eventually your feet... and now open your eyes.

Points to make:

- ✔ Self-belief reinforces your belief that you can do it; that you want to do it. Research shows that positive thinking can have a powerful effect on your achievement.
- ✔ Avoid panic at the beginning of examinations. Concentrating on being relaxed stops the uncomfortable feelings of panic setting in, which can close down the thinking part of the brain. This exercise allows you to begin the exam/revision session in a relaxed, positive state of mind.
- ✔ Talk about the preparation sportsmen/women use for big events. They use relaxation and positive visualisation and talk themselves into feeling they will be successful. Give examples of sportsmen/women who you know do this.

Success comes in cans, failure in can'ts.

Review

> **Aim/s:** To review the skills and information explored in the workshop.
>
> **Resources:** None.

What?

Talk the students back through the workshop – what did we do? In pairs ask the students to recall the tasks they did in the order that they did them.

So what?

So, what was the point of each task?

What now?

Encourage the students to think about how they will be able to use what they have done during the workshop in their own revision and in the run-up to their exams. Ask the students to make decisions about how they will put this into practice – ask them to share these decisions with their group.

> ❛This helped me plan my revision methods!❜
>
> UFA student

'A journey of a thousand miles starts from beneath one's feet.'

From *Tao te ching*

Understanding the exam question -- terms

Analyse	Compare
Illustrate	Outline
State	Summarise
Review	Clarify

Comment on

Consider

Demonstrate

Describe

Discuss

Contrast

Explain

Understanding the exam question – definitions

Look very closely at the detail.

Say how things are the same and different.

Give examples to make your points clear. It can also mean to use diagrams, drawings or figures to support your answer.

Describe without too much detail. Give the main features of.

Present the information clearly but briefly.

Give your opinions or point of view.

Go over the whole thing picking out the important parts to give your opinion on.

Using your own words, bring together the main points without including detail or examples

---

Make it simple and clear

Take into account. What are your thoughts about it?

Show using lots of examples.

Give a detailed account of something as it is. You do not need to give your opinion on it.

Give the important reasons for and against and come to some conclusion from these.

Show how things are different.

Make the information clear by giving reasons for it.

Understanding the exam question –
terms and definitions list

TERMS	DEFINITIONS
Analyse	Look very closely at the detail.
Compare	Say how things are the same and different.
Illustrate	Give examples to make your points clear. It can also mean to use diagrams, drawings or figures to support your answer.
Outline	Describe without too much detail. Give the main features of.
State	Present the information clearly but briefly.
Summarise	Using your own words, bring together the main points without including detail or examples.
Review	Go over the whole thing picking out the important parts to give your opinion on.
Clarify	Make it simple and clear.
Comment on	Give your opinions or point of view.
Consider	Take into account. What are your thoughts about it?
Demonstrate	Show using lots of examples.
Describe	Give a detailed account of something as it is. You do not need to give your opinion on it.
Discuss	Give the important reasons for and against and come to some conclusion from these.
Contrast	Show how things are different.
Explain	Make the information clear by giving reasons for it.

Can you think of any other words often used in exam questions? List them here. What do they mean?

Put a tick against words you feel uncomfortable with. This will help you identify words you need to practise with.

Exam Tips

Get a good night's sleep before the exam.

Always leave ten minutes at the end to read through your work and make any last-minute corrections.

If you are running out of time complete your question in the form of notes.

Read the instructions carefully. Put a tick next to the questions you have to do/want to do.

Where possible, do your best questions first.

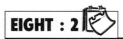
Look out for how many marks a question has – this often tells you how much detail you should include.

Dress for comfort, not just for fashion. Make sure you are able to take a layer of clothing off if you are too hot or put a layer on if you are too cold.

Don't let one bad experience influence how you feel about yourself and exams.

When tackling long questions, plan them first. A mind map is a good way to do this.

Underline the important words in a long question – this will help you break down the question and check you have answered all parts of it.

If your mind goes blank or you feel really stressed and can't think clearly, try some deep breathing exercises.

Get to the exam early.

Make sure you take all the equipment you might need. Think about spare batteries for your calculator. Sharpen your pencil in advance. Gather everything you need the night before.

Don't spend too long on one question. Work out how much time you have for each question at the beginning of the exam and stick to that.

Make sure you attempt all the questions you need to.

Read through the whole paper.

Don't be afraid to write on the exam paper - you might want to underline words in a question or make very quick notes.

Save time – don't repeat yourself when answering a question. You will get no extra marks for saying the same thing twice.

If possible, take a bottle of water and perhaps some sweets with you to the exam room.

Before you set off from home, relax and imagine yourself walking calmly to the exam room and successfully completing the exam. If you see it and believe it, it is more likely to come true.

SUMMARY SHEET – EXAM TIPS

1.   Get a good night's sleep before the exam.

2.   Always leave ten minutes at the end to read through your work and make any last-minute corrections.

3.   If you are running out of time complete your question in the form of notes.

4.   Read the instructions carefully. Put a tick next to the questions you have to do/want to do.

5.   Where possible, do your best questions first.

6.   Look out for how many marks a question has – this often tells you how much detail you should include.

7.   Dress for comfort, not just for fashion. Make sure you are able to take a layer of clothing off if you are too hot or put a layer on if you are too cold.

8.   Don't let one bad experience influence how you feel about yourself and exams.

9.   When tackling long questions, plan them first. A mind map is a good way to do this.

10.   Underline the important words in a long question – this will help you break down the question and check you have answered all parts of it.

11.   If your mind goes blank or you feel really stressed and can't think clearly, try some deep breathing exercises.

12.   Get to the exam early.

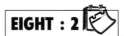
13.   Make sure you take all the equipment you might need. Think about spare batteries for your calculator. Sharpen your pencil in advance. Gather everything you need the night before.

14.   Don't spend too long on one question. Work out how much time you have for each question at the beginning of the exam and stick to that.

15.   Make sure you attempt all the questions you need to.

16.   Read through the whole paper.

17.   Don't be afraid to write on the exam paper - you might want to underline words in a question or make very quick notes.

18.   Save time – don't repeat yourself when answering a question. You will get no extra marks for saying the same thing twice.

19.   If possible, take a bottle of water and perhaps some sweets with you to the exam room.

20.   Before you set off from home, relax and imagine yourself walking calmly to the exam room and successfully completing the exam. If you see it and believe it, it is more likely to come true.

'People will exceed targets they set themselves.'

Gordon Dryden
International broadcaster & author

A quick guide to the UFA

The UFA is a national education charity. Founded in Birmingham in 1996 by Professor Tim Brighouse, it is now working in 34 Local Education Authorities across England.

> *Giving young people more time to do more of the same, in the same way, with the same people is not going to raise standards of achievement dramatically upward – we need to do something radically different.*

Professor Tim Brighouse at the launch of the UFA, April 1996

The UFA has the following defining features:

- **Beyond school**
  The UFA extends the learning of young people beyond the traditional school day by offering learning opportunities before and after school, at weekends and during the holidays.

- **Networked**
  The UFA works with schools and communities to develop home, school and community linked learning programmes. Partner schools and organisations subscribe to the UFA core principles upon entering the partnership and embark on a developmental programme to enhance, extend and enrich the learning of young people.

- **Innovative**
  The UFA is committed to exploring innovative, brain based approaches to learning to boost learner potential and raise achievement.

- **Energetic**
  The UFA is developed by energetic UFA Fellows who come from partner schools and organisations. They take part in training and work together to develop UFA activity in their own organisations and across a local area.

- **Partnership**
  The UFA works at local level, alongside a local UFA manager, to set up partnerships with schools, community groups and other organisations in order to build the local UFA. The UFA is committed to building local capacity and uniting people, young and old, in a common endeavour to release learning potential.

> A production at the West Yorkshire Playhouse, a special edition of the Yorkshire Post, the design of a new strip for Leeds United FC – nothing is beyond the young people who make up UFA Leeds!

Mark Hopkins, Leeds UFA partnership manager

- **Belonging**

  UFA tutors and students from UFA partner schools are brought together with other members of local UFA learning teams to build a sense of identity and a common approach to teaching and learning.

- **Transforming**

  The UFA works with schools to develop experimental, creative approaches to learning that support their commitment to transform teaching and learning for students and teachers.

Do you want to find out more?

Currently the UFA has established partnerships in more than 30 centres around the UK and this number is growing rapidly. Visit our web site at www.ufa.org.uk to find out more about the partnership programme, the work of the UFA and how we can work with you.

email us: ufa_admin@birmingham.gov.uk

Phone us: 0121 202 2347

Fax us: 0121 202 2384

Or write to us:

National UFA

Millennium Point

Curzon Street

Birmingham

B4 7XG

‘UFA has become a pioneer of new ways of learning – not seeking to banish or denigrate existing forms of provision, but reconfiguring resources to gain greater leverage from learning potential. ’

Tom Bentley, DEMOS

Reading list

The reading list below is by no means exhaustive but it's a start! Books marked with ☆ are suggested as a good starting point for those wishing to explore accelerated learning approaches.

	Bellanca, J & Fogarty, R	1986	*Catch Them Thinking*	IRI Skylight, Illinois
☆	Buzan, T	1993	*The Mind Map Book*	BBC Books, London
	Buzan, T	1986	*Use Your Memory*	BBC Books, London
	Call, N & Smith, A	1999	*the alps approach*	Network Educational Press Ltd., Stafford
	De Amicis, B	1999	*Multiple Intelligences Made Easy*	Zephyr Press, Tucson Arizona
	Dryden, G & Vos, J	1994	*The Learning Revolution*	Network Educational Press Ltd., Stafford
	Fletcher, M	1998	*Teaching for Success*	Brain-Friendly Publications Hythe
☆	Fogarty, R	1997	*Brain Compatible Classrooms*	Skylight Professional Development
☆	Gardner, H	1993	*Multiple Intelligences: The Theory in Practice*	Basic Books
☆	Goleman, H	1995	*Emotional Intelligence*	Bloomsbury, London
	Hancock, J	1996	*Have a Mega Memory*	Hodder, London
	Hannaford, C	1995	*Smart Moves*	Great Ocean Publishers, Arlington, Virginia
	Hughes, M	1999	*Closing the Learning Gap*	Network Educational Press Ltd., Stafford
	Hughes, M & Vass, A	2001	*Strategies for Closing the Learning Gap*	Network Educational Press Ltd., Stafford
	Jensen, E	1998	*Teaching with the Brain in Mind*	Turning Point Publishing Del Mar, California
☆	Jensen, E	1996	*Brain-Based Learning*	Turning Point Publishing Del Mar, California
	Jensen, E	1993	*Thirty days to B's and A's*	Turning Point Publishing Del Mar, California
	Lovatt, M & Wise, D	2001	*Creating an Accelerated Learning School*	Network Educational Press Ltd., Stafford
☆	Marguiles, N	1995	*Map It !*	Zephyr Press, Tucson Arizona
☆	Smith, A	1998	*Accelerated Learning in Practice*	Network Educational Press Ltd., Stafford
	Smith, A	1996	*Accelerated Learning in the Classroom*	Network Educational Press Ltd., Stafford

Interesting websites

The following is a list of sites we hope you will find useful – we can't vouch for all the content you could possibly come across from these starting points but there is a fantastic wealth of information and resources on the web. We have included some sites that have a specific revision focus, but also sites with a more general focus on aspects of accelerated learning.

Revision sites

www.bbc.co.uk/schools/gcsebitesize/

The BBC's fantastic revision site. The site itself is really helpful, but the 'hotlinks' section – (www.bbc.co.uk/schools/gcsebitesize/otherstuff/hotlinks/index.shtml) – is absolutely fantastic. Many of the sites below can be found through these links.

www.gcsemaths.fsnet.co.uk/

A good site for maths revision.

www.projectgcse.co.uk/

A nice site for GCSE revision, although the quality of the material varies and some of the subject areas are better covered than others.

www.re-xs.ucsm.ac.uk/gcsere/index.html

An RE revision page.

www.kingston.ac.uk/tlss/revision.htm

A site covering revision strategies in general, which could be used at a variety of levels.

www.positivelymad.co.uk/al/study_skills.htm

A really nice guide to accelerated learning and study skills.

www.learnline.ntu.edu.au/studyskills/ex/ex_ep_re.html

This is a useful guide, particularly in relation to memory techniques. Although some parts of the site are tailored towards university students, much of it is more general.

www.support4learning.org.uk/education/study.htm#revision

A nice revision skills links page.

U.F.A. Brain Friendly Revision

Accelerated Learning sites

www.jspr.btinternet.co.uk/University/Stockton /Lectures/3Multiple/MultiIntelligence.htm	Multiple Intelligence articles.
www.thethinkingclassroom.co.uk	An excellent site, includes an on-line Multiple Intelligence quiz.
www.accelerated-learning-uk.co.uk/method/test_flash.html	A nice online learning styles quiz.
www.mathmatters.net/braingym.htm	Brain Gym®
www.brainconnection.com	A nice site with some good activities and information.
www.mind-map.com	Tony Buzan's mind mapping site.
www.thinks.com	A site with some great brain games and puzzles and an on-line spirograph!
www.newhorizons.org	A site with a huge amount of content – we recommend the Brain Lab.
www.uwsp.edu/education/lwilson/lessons/1mico.htm	A site featuring some Multiple Intelligence lesson plans and links to other Multiple Intelligence sites.
www.MIResearch.org	Dr Charles Branton Shearer's Multiple Intelligences research site – a good source of information.
www.mindmotivation.com	Steve Minshull's site containing a range of ideas about how to use accelerated learning techniques.

Music to aid learning

Research shows that certain types of music can really help you to learn. Play low volume, non lyrical (no words), classical music (ideally around 60 beats per minute) when you are studying and concentrating. It cuts out distracting background noise and increases your subconscious alpha waves, which help you to learn more effectively.

Baroque music from around 1600–1750 is ornamental and simply organised in structure. It builds methodically and much of it has 55–80 beats per minute. However, there are examples of more up-to-date music that fits this description too (see Johnson below), but these may be more difficult to get hold of. There are now many CDs available which have been specifically compiled with learning in mind.

Here are a few examples of pieces of music you might like to use to aid concentration:

Albinoni	*Adagio in G minor*
Corelli	*Concerti Grossi*
Ed Alleyne-Johnson	*Purple Electric Violin Concerto*
Handel	*Water Music*
J.S. Bach	*Brandenburg Concertos (especially nos. 2 & 5)*
Mozart	*Rondeau from flute quartet no. 1 in D major*
Pachelbel	*Canon in D*
Vivaldi	*The Four Seasons*

U.F.A. Brain Friendly Revision

Acknowledgements

The publishers wish to thank the following people and organisations for permission to use extracts from their material in this book. Every effort has been made to contact copyright holders of materials reproduced in this book. The publishers apologise for any omissions and will be pleased to rectify them at the earliest opportunity.

Brain Gym® (see pages 35–7) was developed by Paul & Gayle Dennison. For further information on Brain Gym® or to book a session, contact Educational Kinesiology UK, Kay McCarroll International Faculty, 12 Golder's Rise, Hendon, London NW4 2HR.

The section on mind mapping (pages 113–128) was influenced by and adapted in part from Buzan, T (1995) *The Mind Map Book*, BBC Publications, pages 91–114.

'Using the body to remember' (pages 193–5) 'Remembering words through stories' (pages 147–9) were influenced by and adapted in part from Hancock, J (1996) *Have a Mega Memory*, Hodder Children's Books, pages 13–14.

The quotation from Jensen, E (1996) *Completing the Puzzle: A Brain-Based Approach to Learning* (page 17) is reproduced by permission of The Brain Store, San Diego, CA.

The 'Building a living brain' activity on pages 25–9 was adapted from a training session delivered by Dr. Mark McKergow and is reproduced by permission of Dr. Mark McKergow, Mark McKergow Associates, 26 Christchurch Road, Cheltenham GL50 2PL, UK. www.mckergow.com – Accelerated Learning, Music for Learning.

'One – ten in Japanese' (pages 61–3) is adapted from a workshop held by Steve Minshull." Steve Minshull Mind Motivation Ltd. www.mindmotivation.com.

'Asking positive questions' (page 95) 'What motivates; what de-motivates? It's up to you' (pages 91-93 and 105–6) and 'What are my revision habits?' (pages 91–3) were influenced by and adapted from O'Brien J & B (1996) *Lightening Learning*, Quantum Training UK Ltd., pages 34 and 74.

'Self-relaxation exercise' (page 217–9) was adapted from a workshop held by Dr. Roy Padgett.

The poem 'You can't be that' by Brian Patten (page 4) was reproduced from '*Another Day on your Foot and I would have Died.*' An Anthology of Children's Poetry (1996), Macmillan.

'What motivates; what de-motivates? It's up to you' (pages 105–6), 'What are my revision habits?' (pages 91–3) and 'VAK questionnaire' (pages 171–8 and 177–9) were influenced by and adapted in part from Rose, C (1999) *Master it Faster*, Accelerated Learning Systems Ltd., pages 38–9. Reproduced by permission of Colin Rose, Accelerated Learning Systems Ltd., 50 Aylesbury Road, Aylesbury, Bucks, UK, HP22 5AH.

Activities index

U.F.A. Brain Friendly Revision